the greatest story

BIBLE INTRODUCTION

the greatest story

BIBLE INTRODUCTION

 AUGSBURG FORTRESS

THE GREATEST STORY
BIBLE INTRODUCTION

ISBN: 978-1-4514-0120-2

Writers: Scott Tunseth, Luther Dale (Chapter 1)
Illustrators: David L. Hanson, Julie Lonneman
Cover design: Alisha Lofgren
Interior design: Ivy Palmer Skrade
Typesetting: PerfecType, Nashville, TN

The paper used in this publication meets the minimum requirements of American National Standard for Information Sciences—Permanence of Paper for Printed Library Materials, ANSI Z329.48-1984.

Manufactured in the U.S.A.

13 12 11 10 1 2 3 4 5 6 7 8 9 10

CONTENTS

THE STORY
Introducing
the Bible

The story behind the greatest story

We love stories

- What is one of your favorite stories to tell?

Each of us has a story to tell

- What is a favorite family story? Who first told you that story?

TELL ME A STORY

Whether we are children or adults, we love to hear good stories. They are part of our earliest memories. We are captivated by family stories that tell of our family roots. We are fascinated when our grandparents tell how they met and fell in love. We are excited by stories filled with adventure and mystery, humor or surprise. Who can resist the thrill of entering Harry Potter's world or laughing as Garrison Keillor spins his fanciful tales of Lake Wobegon? So much of what happens in our lives is told through stories. Facts and dates have their place, but we often learn history best through hearing stories about people and events. We love stories because they introduce us to new worlds and people beyond our own. They ignite our imaginations of what the world was once like and what it might yet be.

Everyone has a story. And everyone has a story to tell. We are shaped by our stories, and the stories we remember and tell shape us. Just think, for example, of the many stories behind our digitally stored pictures and photo albums. Our stories connect with, are woven into, the stories of others. These stories are like windows into our total life experience, which includes celebration and loss, joy and pain. Through stories we see more clearly the truth of who we are.

*We can discover our
stories in the "greatest
story"*

- How much do you feel you
know about the Bible, the
greatest story? (Don't worry
if the answer is "little" or
"nothing." We are here to
discover it together.)

And speaking of stories and truth, you are about to experience the "greatest story" of all, the Bible. You will discover what makes it so great: it's a story that helps us make sense of our own stories. The story told in the Bible *is* our story. It includes each one of us. We are part of the greatest story ever told, the big story of God. Though the Bible's story of God began long ago, it continues to unfold in our lives. You are invited into the adventure and mystery of God's big, continuing story. It will ignite your imagination. As you enter God's story, be prepared to be surprised—and forever changed.

THE BIBLE HAS A STORY, TOO

How the Bible came to be is a pretty fascinating story in itself. We sometimes call the Bible God's book, but God didn't write it or drop it from the sky. God inspired people to write the stories, prayers, laws, letters, and all the rest found in the Bible. So even though we say the Bible is inspired by God, it was written by people, many different people writing at different times and places spanning nearly one thousand years!

*The Bible developed
gradually over nearly
1000 years*

- What, if anything, were you
taught about how the Bible
came to be?

The Bible has been around for a long time as a single book, but that's not how it all started.

One of the reasons it took so long for the Bible to become one book is that it really is a collection of books. The word *bible* actually comes from a Greek word that means "the books." The Bible is like a library. Each of the books in some way expresses experiences of God's presence and activity in the Jewish community (Old Testament) and the Christian community (New Testament). In other words, no one author decided one day to write a Bible. The Bible came together over a long time.

*The Bible was told
before it was written*

- Early in your life, were you
told stories from the Bible?
If so, which ones? Who told
these stories to you?

Much of the Bible was spoken before it was written down. Imagine sitting around a campfire being told the story of how God created the world, or how the young shepherd boy David took down the giant enemy named Goliath with his little slingshot. That is how the Jewish people first told stories of their encounters with the living God. They prayed prayers, sang songs of joy and sadness, and shared wisdom with each other. Eventually, the stories and all the different writings found in the Old Testament were written down, but it took centuries for all the books to make it into print. And those first manuscripts weren't like our books. They were written on scrolls made of animal skins or reed paper.

Even the stories about Jesus (see the Gospels of Matthew, Mark, Luke, and John) were told by word of mouth for decades before being written down. After Jesus' death and resurrection around 30 C.E. (A.D.*), his life and his teachings were remembered and first passed along orally by his followers. No reporters recorded eyewitness accounts of Jesus during his lifetime. Eventually, the early Christians realized they needed to preserve what Jesus said and did, so they started writing this down. The first writings of the New Testament were actually the letters of the apostle Paul (written in the 50s C.E.), not the Gospels (written between 70 and 90 C.E.). The last books of the New Testament were likely written in the early second century.

Eventually, the Hebrew Scriptures—what Christians call the Old Testament—were gathered into collections of scrolls. And the Christian community eventually gathered the individual books and letters being used by different churches into a single list or *canon*. The canon was a list of accepted writings that became authoritative for the life and faith of the Christian community. But coming up with this final list was not easy. The process went on for nearly three hundred years. In an Easter letter written in 367 C.E., a bishop name Athanasius offered a list of twenty-seven books to be considered as having authority for faith and life. Even though the debate continued, the twenty-seven books he named are the ones still included in the New Testament.

If you compare Bibles today, you might find that they don't all contain the same number of books. Protestant, Catholic, and Orthodox Bibles differ somewhat in the number of Old Testament books. Protestant Bibles usually have 39 Old Testament books and 27 New Testament books. Roman Catholic and Orthodox Bibles include some additional books known as the Apocrypha. Martin Luther included the apocryphal books in a separate section of his translation of the Bible in the sixteenth century. He said these books were good to read, but did not have the same authority as the 39 books included in the Jewish canon.

- Who is the best storyteller you know?

A canon (list) of authoritative New Testament books was proposed in 367 C.E.

- How do writings or public documents become authoritative? Why do you think some books made it into the Bible and others did not?

* Dates can be designated by two different sets of initials. The traditional B.C. ("before Christ") is the same as B.C.E. (Before the Common Era). The abbreviation A.D. stands for the Latin phrase *anno domini* ("in the year of our Lord") and is the equivalent of C.E. (Common Era). Christians have used A.D. and B.C. to call attention to the importance of Christ's incarnation and to center human history around this event. However, many Bible scholars and study Bibles today use the B.C.E. and C.E. abbreviations.

The Bible is God's powerful book

• What book or story has been powerful, even life-changing, for you? Why?

The Old Testament tells of God's promises to the people of Israel

• How do you imagine God? Is God "out there"? Is God "here"? What difference does it make?

At the center of the New Testament is Jesus Christ

• How would you describe the power of words? Can you think of a time when spoken or written words really affected you?

THE BIBLE IS GOD'S STORY

The Bible is God's book. It powerfully and beautifully tells the story of God's actions and God's relationship with humanity and all creation. God speaks to us through songs of praise and lament, the beauty of poetry, the stories of history, the insight of wisdom, and the confrontations of the prophets. The story of God becomes for us the powerful Word of God. That Word is full of demand and judgment, forgiveness and hope. It is a Word that sets us free to love and serve. It is a Word that inspires trust and faith in Jesus Christ. Christians say that the Bible is God's story centered around Jesus Christ. In Christ we see most clearly the character and heart of God.

The Old and New Testaments are two parts of the larger story of God. Both are about God's relationship with the world and humankind. In the Old Testament, the focus is on the people of Israel and the promises God made to them. God chooses and blesses a people, so all the world can be blessed through them. God patiently put up with the people in spite of their complaints, disobedience, and lack of faith. God sent prophets to call the people back into a relationship with God. The Old Testament story reveals how the people of Israel lived between the tension of sin and the hope of salvation.

The New Testament continues this story of God's loving relationship with humanity. At the center are the stories of Jesus, God's Son. He reveals God's love and divine power through his teaching, preaching, and miracles. God's love and fullness are seen in the life, death, and resurrection of Jesus. In him God overcomes evil and death to bring new life for the present and everlasting life to come.

Before Jesus left this earth to be with God, he promised to send the Holy Spirit to the early Christians, so they would have the courage to tell the good news of Jesus. With the Spirit's power, they preached and performed signs and wonders. Eventually, followers of Jesus, such as the apostle Paul, wrote down what they were inspired to say about Jesus. These writings were copied and read among the churches. As people heard these writings, they seemed to be the powerful words of God speaking to them.

The Bible emerged as authoritative because it created faith and empowered a new way of life—a life energized by love—in those who heard it and lived it.

THE BIBLE IS OUR STORY

The Bible is the story of God's desire to be in relationship with us humans, so it is also a story about the people of God. And who are the people of God, exactly? To answer that, you have to go all the way back to the beginning, to the moment of creation. The Bible makes it clear that God created all things, including human beings. That means that every person who has ever lived can claim to come from God. Genesis boldly confesses that people are created in the image of God. That means we share God's creative and life-giving concern for creation and for one another.

The Bible is about real people

But the Bible also reminds us of the other side of the coin. People are flawed. God is perfect, but we are not. We are complicated and confounding. The Bible talks about this as sin. From Adam and Eve on, we all are touched by sin. So, our story always includes both blessing and sin. The Bible draws us into the drama of stories about real people like us. We see mirror images of ourselves and what the world is like. The people we meet in the Bible are not perfect. They are both heroically faithful and painfully unfaithful.

- Who is one of the most interesting people you have ever met? Why?

Through the stories and people of the Bible, we see the way the world really is. We see people just like us who face difficulties, struggle, and ask questions. They are self-absorbed as well as self-giving. They worship God and forget God while going their own way. We hear the stories of communities of faith figuring out how to live together in justice and peace. We see individuals struggle to be faithful to God. The Bible tells our story as we encounter real people and human communities in all their diversity and complexity.

People in the Bible are both heroically faithful and painfully unfaithful

The Bible is our story because it's about our human response to God's love and hope for us in the world. It's the ongoing story of God choosing ordinary, complicated, and imperfect people like us to do God's work in the world. We hear echoes of our own words in people who wonder, suffer, question, trust, hear, and respond to God's work of faith in them. The Bible is a book of faith, about people who become the people of God.

- What are some human behaviors that illustrate that we are complicated beings?

We are invited to make the Bible our story

What are some of the biggest barriers preventing God's story from continuing into the next generation?

The Bible is our story because God's story is ongoing, and we are called to continue it. In the Bible we see colorful people in vibrant faith communities who are mentors and models for us. Their voices encourage us to become today's people of God. It is in God becoming human in Jesus Christ that we have a picture of what this might look like for us. Our story connects fully with God's story as we respond to God's Spirit to live and act in faith as the people of God. We are called by God to live our story inside God's story. In this way, the Bible is also a very human book.

YOUR PART IN THE GREATEST STORY

The stories of the Bible await you. The Bible explores the mysteries of who God is and how God acts in the world. From generation to generation, the greatest story has asked and answered the biggest questions of life: Who are we? Where do we come from? Who do we belong to? What is the purpose of life? How should we live? The Bible expresses awe and wonder at the power of God who creates and sustains life in the world. It tells the big story of God who keeps on loving us, no matter what. It tells the stories of people like us who yearn for the presence of God, for healing, and for peace.

Bring your questions to the story

- What is your biggest question about God? What is your biggest question about life?

No prior understanding of the Bible is required

- What do you think is the biggest barrier for you in reading and understanding the Bible?

Consider where you fit in the greatest story

Have you ever thought that you have a faith story worth telling? What would help you to tell your faith story?

You are invited to see where you fit in the greatest story and how the greatest story fits in your life. Don't worry if you know little or nothing about the Bible. Set aside your fears that the Bible is overwhelming and too difficult to understand. No prior experience or special training is needed. Just bring an open mind and heart. God's Spirit will be present to help you hear God's Word speak through the Bible and through the words of others who are here with you.

So, get ready to enter the story and meet the living God who is already here. Get ready to imagine how the greatest story can come alive for you, as you hear the great stories of faith and as you tell your own story.

Background Files (Lutheran Study Bible)

Review the timeline on pages 30-32. Notice how many years are covered by the events in the Bible. Then consider that the writings that make up the Bible were written over hundreds of years. What other books or other records were created over such a long period?

Notice the two photos on page 22. In what languages were the Old and New Testaments written? Modern Bibles are based on translating these ancient manuscripts.

Take a look at the chart called "Different Canons of the Hebrew Bible (Old Testament)" on pages 28-29. It's quite complicated. Don't worry if you don't understand all the terms or notes on these pages. What's the main difference you see between the four lists of books?

PICTURING THE STORY

As you watch artist Joe Castillo picture the story of how the Bible came to be, reflect on these questions:

- What, if anything, has surprised you about how the Bible came to be? Does this change the way you think about the Bible? If so, in what way?
- What more would you like to know about how the Bible came to be?
- In what way is the Bible God's book? In what way is it a human book?
- Name two or three themes that you think are going to be pretty important in the greatest story.
- What fears or concerns do you bring to reading and studying the Bible?
- How do you imagine yourself in the greatest story? How do you imagine the greatest story in you?

SINGING AND PRAYING THE STORY

The book of Psalms found in the Bible was the worship book of the people of Israel. The psalms are prayers and songs used to offer praise and thanks to God, ask for God's help, seek God's forgiveness, remember God's actions, and even complain or cry out to God. Christians use the psalms the very same way as we worship and as we reflect on our relationship with God.

Psalm 119:73-80; 105-112

A psalm celebrating God for creating human beings and giving us the law for reflection and guidance.
Notice how the truths of the law are positive for life and given in love by God.

Psalm 29

A psalm that embraces God as a God who speaks.
How does the writer convey that when God speaks, people listen? Is God's voice still heard in the same ways today?

MARK IT

Choose one or more of the following stories to read during the coming week. Mark your reading using the marking method shown here.

1 Samuel 3:1-19	Luke 16:19-31
Micah 4:1-5	Romans 5:6-11

Marking Your Bible

Make notes about the questions and insights you have as you read your Bible. The following symbols might be helpful.

* ∗ A chapter or verse important to me
* ! A new idea
* √ A passage to memorize
* ? Something not clear to me
* ∞ God's love
* ⑫ A promise from God
* ≈ Something that connects with my experience
* † My relationship with God
* ↔ My relationships with others

Next Time

In Chapter 2 you will begin to explore the greatest story at the beginning with the stories in Genesis. To help you review this week's story and prepare for the next chapter, you are encouraged to read the following pieces from *Lutheran Study Bible:*

* Introduction to the Bible, pages 19-29
* Old Testament Overview, pages 41-43
* Pentateuch Introduction, pages 45-46
* Genesis Introduction, pages 47-48

BEGINNINGS
Genesis

A God-created world . . . a God-formed people . . .
two beginnings

God created

- How do you see the stories of creation fitting with modern scientific theories about how the world was created?

And God said, "It's all good!"

- What's the most amazing thing to you about the world we live in?

God created humans from the earth for the earth

- What do you think it means that people were called to "keep" the earth (2:15)?

care for it.

CREATION! (Genesis 1)

The Bible begins at the beginnings. "In the beginning when *God created . . . .*" Right in the very first sentence of the Bible we run into a key statement about what we believe about God and matters of faith. Who created the world and everything in it? God. The beautiful stories in Genesis 1 and 2—about the creation of the universe, the earth, and all its inhabitants— are faith stories. Not science lessons. Not what we call history today. Faith stories.

You've probably heard the phrase, "It's all good!" Well, it was, according to God. That refrain appears over and over in Genesis 1: "God saw that it was good." Even the first human beings, our ancestors, were made in God's own image (1:27), and God gave the world to them as a gift. When you think about it, isn't this remarkable little planet floating in the vast universe still a wondrous place? Do we think of it as a gift?

Now, you might be thinking, *we* look at the world differently than those who wrote Genesis over 2,500 years ago or so. We know a lot more about the origins of the world—or at least we think we do. What about the Big Bang Theory, evolution, dinosaurs, or Ice Ages? How does Genesis fit with all that?

People have differing opinions about when the world began and how long it took to become the world we know and experience. Generally, our key faith statements don't try to explain these things. Science can give us some insights. Genesis, however, emphasizes the "who" of creation. God created. And God gifted. Thanks be to God!

God is God and we aren't

- Describe your understanding of the relationship between Creator and creation (including human beings).

Sin is turning away from God and in on ourselves

- Where do you see signs of the "upward fall" in the world? How can you stay "grounded" in your relationship with God? With others?

FALLING UP (Genesis 2–4)

Creation was filled with good things, including a garden, which contained a tree called "the tree of the knowledge of good and evil" (Genesis 2:17). That tree came with a warning: Eating this fruit causes death!

This seems like a strange thing to put in the good garden. But there it was. And just to make sure the people didn't forget about it, a serpent kept reminding Eve and Adam about the fruit on that most special tree. What made it so special? Well, eating its fruit could open a person's eyes as wide as God's eyes. And God could see, and God knew, everything.

How could seeing through God's eyes be a bad thing? After all, humans were made in God's image. Why not take the next step up? So Eve and Adam reached up for the fruit that would take them to the next level, and they ate. They had committed the first sin, sometimes called "the Fall." But their fall was an upward one. They tried to be like God; more than that, they wanted to be God.

It was the beginning of the end, the end of life in the garden as they had known it. They had to exit the garden and make a life for themselves on the outside looking in. As bad as it looked, God was still taking care of them, giving them clothes and the means to grow food.

It wasn't long before the consequences of their sin hit home. One of their sons—Cain—didn't like it when God gave his brother Abel's offering more attention. In a jealous rage, Cain killed his brother. Beat him to death right there in the field in front of God. Hard to believe, except when we look around and see that story reenacted every day. Hard to deny the power of sin in our lives.

Sin is the inability to fear, love, and trust God. We turn away from God and in on ourselves. We seek our own will first, and we use the gifts of creation, including other people, to gratify our own desires. It's why God acted in Christ Jesus to make us aware of our sin and our need to repent. Only then can we have a renewed vision of ourselves and our world. But that's getting way ahead of the story!

DO OVER! (Genesis 6–9)

The "fall up" turned out to be the start of a bad slide down. A number of generations of human beings populated the earth and some even got involved with the "sons of God" (Nephilim). The human race was so wicked it became unbearable to God. God needed a mulligan, a do-over, so God had a man named Noah build a big—really big—lifeboat. An ark.

Noah was a righteous man who stood out in the sewer of sinful neighbors. So, Noah and his family got a ticket on the ark, and so did pairs of all the other creatures in the world. When the doors were shut and sealed, the rain began to fall, and fall. You've probably seen it rain pretty hard before. But this was serious rain. Endless rain. So much rain that the world and all its inhabitants outside the ark were drowned.

When the rain finally stopped and the water started to go down, the big lifeboat rested on a mountain. Noah opened the doors and let creation start its do-over. And God made a huge promise, a promise as wide as the rainbow sign that stretched across the horizon. He made a deal, a covenant, with Noah and all living creatures for generations to come: "I'll never flood the earth like that again!"

The Bible is not the only place that reports a big flood like this one. It's a common story in cultures around the world. It's not hard to imagine world-changing catastrophes. Movie makers use special effects to picture earth's destruction all the time. And headlines warn us that we human beings are changing the face of the earth moment by moment—and not always for the better. Even so, since the doors of the ark opened, the sun has come up each and every day.

God needed a do-over

- What do you think of God's "do-over"?

But never again . . . that's a promise!

- What does God's commitment to all nonhuman creatures mean for us?
- How do you think we are doing caring for the gift of the earth?

A PROMISING START

(Genesis 12:1—25:18)

The sun was coming up every day, and people began to populate the world once again. The Bible gives the names of many generations up to the family of a man named Terah, who had a son named Abram. Abram married a woman named Sarai. They lived in

Ur of the Chaldeans. That was somewhere in Mesopotamia, or modern-day Iraq.

God formed a people . . . a second "beginning"

- What do you think it means to be "called" by God?

asked or summoned by God

A crazy thing happened next. God *called* Abram and Sarai and asked them to leave their home and take a long journey to a place called Canaan. Why Canaan? Seems God wanted Abram and Sarai to make a new beginning. But that was not all.

God has a habit of making and keeping promises in the Bible. And God made one of the biggest of all to Abram and Sarai. God promised them many descendants and a land to live in. That was no small promise. They were getting very old, and they didn't have any children. Here's the part that may be craziest of all—Abram and Sarai went for it. They believed God and went. That took nerve—and faith.

God promised a big family, a land to live in, many blessings

- What promises affect or shape your life?
- What do you think the phrase "Blessed to be a blessing" meant to Abram and Sarai and their family? What does it mean for you?

Abram's faith became an example of faith throughout the whole Bible (see Romans 4). This was the beginning of blessing for all the world. God promised that, too—that through Abram and Sarai and their family, all the world would be blessed.

It was not a simple road they traveled. Abram almost gave away God's promise when he loaned out Sarai to an Egyptian ruler. When they got tired of waiting to have their own baby, Sarai told Abram to try to have one with their servant Hagar. But when little Ishmael was born to Hagar, Sarai sent them away. Then when God did give Sarai and Abram a child (Isaac) in their old age, God asked Abram to sacrifice his only son—to kill Isaac in the name of God as a gift. That was a big "What?" But Abram faithfully made the arrangements. He was as close as a knife blade from killing Isaac when God stopped him.

A tested faith

- Name the ways Abram and Sarai's faith was tested. How would you define "faith"?

1 *moving to a new place*
2 *sacrificing their son*
3 *depriving them of children for a long time.*

Along the way, Abram and Sarai were given new names—Abraham and Sarah. They had a new land and a son and the promise of many descendants. God's "first family" was ready to grow.

FAMILY FEUD (Genesis 25:19—36:43)

Have you ever thought that maybe people in the Bible were perfect, or at least better than the rest of us? If so, you probably haven't heard this part of the story yet. Abraham and Sarah's children and grandchildren were quite a crew. Their son Isaac had twin sons with his wife Rebekah. The boys, Esau and Jacob, starting feuding right from the start, right in their mother's womb! And when Esau was born first, brother Jacob was grabbing him by the heel. Because he was born first, Esau was in line for his father's birthright, the main share of the family fortune.

Rebekah favored Jacob, while Isaac favored Esau. When the boys grew up, Jacob tricked Esau into handing over the birthright. And Rebekah helped Jacob trick Isaac into receiving his father's blessing. There's that word again—<u>blessing</u>. The blessing given to Abraham and Sarah would continue through Jacob's side of the family. Esau became the head of another big family, and was blessed as well. His descendants would later show up as people of Edom.

Jacob's adventures were far from over. He wanted to marry a girl named Rachel, but her father Laban tricked him into marrying Rachel's older sister first. How did Laban do that? Check it out in Genesis 29. Eventually Jacob did marry Rachel too, and took his growing family and a bunch of livestock from his father-in-law and set off to settle down back in Canaan. Along the way, he wrestled with God, made up with his brother Esau, and had lots of children (including 12 sons) with two wives and two servants. God also repeated the family promises to Jacob and gave him a new name—Israel.

God's promises at work in real people

- Does it surprise you that God's promises got worked out through family members who feuded, tricked one another, and even lied to get what they wanted? Why or why not?

Jacob is named Israel

- God promised Jacob: "I am with you and will keep you wherever you go . . ." (28:15). How might this promise relate to your life?

GOD'S DREAMER (Genesis 37–50)

God's first family with father Jacob (Israel) was growing. And the feuding wasn't done yet! You'd expect some scuffles breaking out amongst twelve brothers, but one particular fight was a game-changer.

Joseph, one of Jacob's youngest sons, started it all. Seems Joseph had become his father Israel's favorite. He even got a long fancy robe from his father.

Joseph's dream lands him in Egypt

- How would you describe the way God was at work in Joseph?
- How would you say God is at work in you?

Don't think the brothers didn't notice. Little Joseph was also a dreamer. He dreamed that his brothers would one day bow to him as their superior. He could've kept that dream to himself, but that wasn't Joseph's style. He told his brothers what he had dreamed. Bad idea.

The brothers resented Joseph, threw him down a well, and would have killed him, if it weren't for brother Reuben. He talked them out of killing Joseph. Good idea. Instead, they sold him to a band of traders passing through on their way to Egypt. The traders sold Joseph to Potiphar, an official of the Egyptian ruler or Pharaoh.

Joseph's dream interpretations save Egypt and his family

Joseph did a fine job as a servant in Potiphar's house. But soon Potiphar's wife took notice of the handsome young man and tried to coax Joseph into an affair. Joseph refused, so she accused him of trying to seduce her. That landed him in jail. That's where Joseph did some serious dream interpretation for two other inmates. He listened to their dreams and told them what they meant. It was bad news for one (Pharaoh's baker) and good news for the other (Pharaoh's cupbearer). The baker was hanged, but the cupbearer got his old job back. When Pharaoh started having weird dreams, the cupbearer told him about Joseph. Good idea.

Joseph interpreted Pharaoh's dreams and was right on target. Pharaoh promoted him to a position of authority in charge of Egypt's food storage program, which saved the land when a bad drought hit. The same drought was hitting Canaan too, so Jacob (Israel) sent his sons to Egypt to beg for food. Guess who they had to bow down to and beg for help? They didn't recognize grown-up Joseph in his Egyptian uniform, but he recognized them.

God can turn bad to good

- In what ways can bad circumstances be used for good? Have you ever experienced something like that?

Joseph could have taken his revenge for the well incident, but he didn't. He helped his brothers with food and eventually revealed to them who he was. He even invited his father Israel and the whole clan to live in Egypt because of the famine. He told his startled brothers: "You intended to harm me, but God intended it for good, in order to preserve many people." And that included the whole family of Israel. The promises of God were alive and well.

Review the timeline on pages 30–32 in *Lutheran Study Bible*. Everything that happens in Genesis 1:1—11:26 is considered Prehistory. We generally don't assign dates to Prehistory. We aren't certain about when God called Abram and Sarai, but we can identify approximate dates for this based on a little clearer knowledge of when later events happened.

Take a look at the map called "The Ancient Near East and Key Locations in Genesis" on page 2098 of *Lutheran Study Bible*. Trace the journeys of Abraham and Sarah. Note the relationship between Canaan and Egypt. Keep in mind that the family of Jacob (Israel) was in Egypt at the close of the book of Genesis.

PICTURING THE STORY

As you watch artist Joe Castillo picture the stories of Genesis, reflect on these questions:

- What part of the story stands out to you?
- In what ways is God at work in the story of beginnings?
- What part of the story do you want to know more about?
- If you could meet any person introduced in the story, who would it be? Why?

SINGING AND PRAYING THE STORY

The book of Psalms found in the Bible was the worship book of the people of Israel. The psalms are prayers and songs used to offer praise and thanks to God, ask for God's help, seek God's forgiveness, remember God's actions, and even complain or cry out to God. Christians use the psalms the very same way as we worship and as we reflect on our relationship with God.

Psalm 8
A creation psalm that praises God as creator of heaven and earth.
Notice how the psalm connects with the story of beginnings.

Psalm 32
A prayer confessing sin and asking for forgiveness.
With which parts of the story does this psalm connect?

MARK IT

Choose one or more of the following passages from today's section of the story to read during the coming week. Mark your reading using the marking method shown here.

Genesis 1:1—2:4

Genesis 15:1-21

Genesis 22:1-19

Genesis 41:1-57

Marking Your Bible

Make notes about the questions and insights you have as you read your Bible. The following symbols might be helpful.

*   A chapter or verse important to me
!   A new idea
√   A passage to memorize
?   Something not clear to me
∞   God's love
ℙ   A promise from God
≈   Something that connects with my experience
†   My relationship with God
↔   My relationships with others

Next Time

In the next chapter we will see and hear about God's people on the move. To review this week's story and to help prepare for the next chapter, you are encouraged to read the following pieces from *Lutheran Study Bible*:

*   Pentateuch Introduction, pages 45-46
*   Genesis Introduction, pages 47-48
*   Exodus Introduction, pages 124-125
*   Leviticus Introduction, pages 189-191
*   Numbers Introduction, pages 237-238
*   Deuteronomy Introduction, pages 302-303

GOD'S PEOPLE ON THE MOVE
Exodus–Deuteronomy

A freedom leader . . . a gift of law . . . and a long journey home

Moses is born!

- Moses survived because of the bravery and compassion of his mother, his sister Miriam, and Pharaoh's own daughter. Who helps you "survive"?

BASKET BABY (Exodus 1–2)

At the end of Genesis, the portion of the story told in chapter 2, the people of Israel were happy to find food and a welcoming land in northeast Egypt, also known as Goshen. It started to feel like home. They put down roots and started to grow their families. But good things sometimes come to an end. Eventually a new Egyptian Pharaoh arose, and he didn't know and didn't care about what Joseph, the son of Israel, had done to save Egypt from famine many decades earlier. This Pharaoh saw the growing family of Israel, the Hebrew people, as a threat. He put them to work as slaves and even tried to kill off their newborn sons. A brave Hebrew mother hid her baby boy Moses in a basket on the river.

God works in strange ways. Pharaoh's own daughter found the baby, adopted him, and took him to live in Pharaoh's house and play right in his back yard. Moses grew up as part of Pharaoh's Egyptian family, but one day his Hebrew blood boiled over when he saw an Egyptian beating a Hebrew. He killed the Egyptian and ran far away to a place called Midian.

BURNING BUSH (Exodus 3–4)

In Midian, Moses married the daughter of a local priest and sheep herder named Jethro. Midian was a long way from Egypt, too far for Moses to hear the cries of his enslaved Hebrew relatives. But God heard the cries, and Moses was about to hear from God. God *does* work in strange ways. While Moses was out herding sheep for Jethro, he heard a voice coming from a burning bush. What a holy hot spot that was! God was speaking, and Moses listened.

Moses is called!

- Imagine you were Moses and heard God calling you to go back to Egypt. What questions would you have for God? What would convince you to go?
- Have you ever experienced God's presence? If so, what was it like? Where did it happen?

Moses will lead!

- Who has been your "Aaron" when you really needed him or her?

"I am the God of your father, the God of Abraham, the God of Isaac, and the God of Jacob." The God who made promises to Abraham and all his descendants was speaking to Moses. If Moses had wondered about his family connections before, God was clearing up any doubts. But that's not all that God had to say. God had heard the cries and prayers of the Hebrew people back in Egypt. And now God wanted Moses to go back to Egypt and negotiate with Pharaoh, to talk him into letting the Hebrew people go home to Canaan.

Moses must have thought: "Negotiate with Pharaoh? You mean the guy who has a murder warrant out on me? The guy who uses the Hebrew slaves to do all the dirty work that needs to be done in Egypt?" Moses was unsure. He didn't think much of his own powers of persuasion. A minor issue, God assured him. God would give him the power to do some miraculous things, which would come in handy when the Egyptian magicians started doing their tricks. Moses' brother Aaron would help with the speechmaking. Most importantly, God would be with Moses.

So Moses and Aaron made the long trip back to Egypt and gave the Hebrew people the first really good news they had heard in a long time. God had heard their pain, and God was about to bring relief!

LET GO, PHARAOH! (Exodus 5–13)

Imagine the scene. Murder suspect Moses gets a meeting with Pharaoh, the ruler of all of Egypt. Foregoing the diplomatic chitchat, Moses gets right to it: "Pharaoh, the God of Israel wants the people of Israel out of Egypt." The look on Pharaoh's face must have said it all. "What?! Let my best slaves go? You're kidding, right? You and your God are nobodies to me. Nobody's going anywhere! Not only that, but I'm going to double the work those slaves are doing right now."

Not the start Moses had hoped for. In fact, he complained to God: "Why did you send me back here? Now the people have it even worse!" God reassured him. God would convince Pharaoh. The people would be free.

Moses and Aaron stuck with it and went back to Pharaoh again. When Pharaoh said no, Moses and Aaron warned that God wasn't kidding. When Pharaoh said no again and again, God sent a bunch of nasty plagues—ten to be exact. A stinking bloody river, swarms of gnats and frogs, big body boils, crop-eating locusts, just to name a few. Still, hard-hearted Pharaoh said no.

The last plague was the game-breaker. God commanded the people of Israel to put the blood of a slaughtered lamb on the doors of their homes. The lamb was part of the meal of remembrance the people were commanded to eat the night before they left Egypt. Then God sent an angel of death across the land. It "passed over" the homes of the Israelite people because of the blood on the doors. (That is why this event is called the Passover.) But the first-born in the homes of the Egyptians died, including Pharaoh's own first-born son. Pharaoh had finally seen enough. He let go and let God lead the people out of Egypt.

The Passover meal of remembrance (the *seder*) is still celebrated in Jewish homes every year. Passover happens close to the time of the most holy Christian days of Maundy Thursday, Good Friday, and Easter. The saving blood of the Passover is often compared to the blood of the crucified Jesus. The Gospel of John in the New Testament reports that Jesus was crucified on the day before Passover, when the Passover lambs were sacrificed (John 19:14, 31). According to other Gospels, the Last Supper was a celebration of Passover (Mark 14:12-16; Luke 22:7-15).

Ten plagues and out!

- The plagues are described in Exodus 7–12. See also the chart summarizing the plagues (*Lutheran Study Bible*, p. 135). Why do you think it took so much to get Pharaoh to change his mind?

Remember Passover

- Why do you think the night the angel of death passed over is remembered in a special meal?
- What events do we tend to celebrate or remember regularly?

THROUGH THE SEA AND BEYOND (Exodus 14–18)

The people could have headed straight northeast toward Canaan by way of the land of the Philistines. But because of the threat of war with the Philistines, God led the people southeast by way of the wilderness toward the Red Sea. What a sight it must have been. The people carrying whatever they could get in their backpacks, walking behind a pillar of cloud during the day and pillar of fire at night.

By the time the people were camped near the Red Sea, Pharaoh had changed his mind. He sent his army to bring the slaves back. When the people saw the dust of Pharaoh's big army approaching, they lost their nerve and complained to Moses and to God: "Did you bring us out of Egypt just to get us slaughtered here by the Egyptian army?" Hard to blame them. There didn't seem to be any way to escape.

Moses showed remarkable calm and promised that God would fight for the people. God did better than that. God told Moses to stretch out his walking staff and hold it toward the sea. Strong winds pushed the waters back, so the people could walk right through it to the other shore. When they were safe, the wind stopped, and the waters fell back together, just as Pharaoh's army was passing through. All the soldiers and their horses were drowned.

After a brief celebration on shore, led by Moses' sister Miriam, the people kept marching through the wilderness. When water and food turned scarce, the people complained again. And again, God listened. God provided water, quail, and a strange food called manna, which covered the ground every morning like dew.

The people were a high-maintenance bunch. They complained, quarreled, and tested Moses and God all along the way. Life in the wilderness was messy and unruly.

God frees by the sea

- What thoughts or questions do you have about what happened at the Red Sea?

God provides in the wilderness

- The manna God provided was to be eaten each day and not stored. There was always enough. How does this vision of everyone having enough compare to or contrast with our eating habits and distribution of food?
- How do you keep going when things are not going right?

I AM THE Lord YOUR GOD

(Exodus 19–40)

The journey through the wilderness included a stop at a place called Mount Sinai. It turned out to be one of the holiest places of all. At Sinai God gave the holy *Torah* or "teaching" to the people. What did God teach there? Well, it was new agreement, a covenant, based on some commandments and rules for living that set them apart as God's people. Part of the covenant was the Ten Commandments, the basics for faithful living in relationship to God and neighbors.

But the even the commandments flowed from God's promise: "I am the Lord your God, who brought you out of the land of Egypt" (Exodus 20:2). Life as God's people began with this confession:

> The God who created heaven and earth,
> the God who called our ancestors Abraham and Sarah
>   and promised them land and many descendants,
> the God who saved us from slavery in Egypt,
> that same God is calling us to trust in God alone
>   and live as holy people.

Moses gave the people the Commandments and many other rules and rituals to live by. At one point when Moses was away for a while, the people lost their nerve again and made a golden statue to worship. Even Moses' brother Aaron helped with that. Right off the bat they broke the very first Commandment: You shall have no other gods before me.

Moses was angry and God punished the people, but when the dust settled, Moses continued to describe how God wanted the people to live together. And together they made a *tabernacle*, the holy tent of God; appointed priests to take care of worship and sacrifices; and even made special garments for those who would serve as priests. The family of Israel, the wandering slaves who left Egypt, were becoming God's holy people.

God's new teaching at Sinai

- The Ten Commandments are listed in Exodus 20:1-17. They are also summarized on a chart on p. 154 of *Lutheran Study Bible*. Why do you think they are sometimes called a "gift" from God?
- What's the most important thing you have ever been taught? Why?

God's holy people

- How would you describe what it means to be a holy person, or part of God's holy people?

GOD IN THE CENTER (Leviticus and Numbers)

Sinai set the stage for the rest of Israel's journey home. All along the way, the people were to keep God at the center of their life together. The people built an ornate box called an *ark of the covenant* for the Ten Commandments. Members of the families assigned to be priests carried the ark ahead of the people whenever they moved from place to place. And when they camped in a place for a while, the ark was placed right in the center of the tabernacle. And the tabernacle was set up right in the middle of camp, with all the different tribal families living in assigned campsites around it.

The book of Leviticus tells how God called out to Moses from the sacred tent and gave him even more laws and regulations for the people. This included a whole system of sacrifices and offerings, rites related to Israel's priests, and many laws related to being ritually pure. Many of these laws seem strange to us, and they can make Leviticus a difficult book to read. But the laws and rituals had a clear purpose: Israel was to maintain its identity as God's "holy people."

Sadly, the people did not always keep God in the center of their hearts and minds. The journey back home to Canaan could have been rather quick, if it weren't for another case of bad nerves. Moses had sent some spies ahead to check out the land of promise (Canaan), but most of the spies, except for two (Joshua and Caleb), said the people living there were too much of a threat. It wasn't worth the risk. The lack of nerve cost the people dearly. God said that a whole generation would die in the wilderness and not make it back home. Nearly 40 more years of wandering in the wilderness lay ahead.

The book of Numbers tells much about this time in the wilderness. Horrible things can happen to people, even when God is in their midst. The stories in Numbers teach us something about how to follow by waiting for God to lead. The tribes of Israel were counted and were becoming more organized, but they also faced internal rebellions and battles with other peoples along the way. They reached the east side of the Jordan River, and started to think about how to divide up the promised land amongst the tribes.

An identity based on relationship, rules, and rituals

- How do you keep God at the center of your life?

Fear leads to 40 more years!

- What is the most difficult thing you have ever faced? How did you face it?
- What, in your opinion, is hard about waiting for God to lead?

KEEP THESE WORDS (Deuteronomy)

As the people were preparing to enter the promised land of Canaan, Moses gathered them for some serious conversation. Well, he did most of the talking. In fact, Moses delivered a number of speeches. He reviewed all that had happened to the people while wandering in the wilderness. He reminded them about the Ten Commandments, and encouraged them to obey God's law. He urged the people to teach God's words to every generation: "You should even tie God's word to your arms and foreheads," he said. Moses repeated all the laws that the people needed to follow once they arrived in Canaan, and he warned them of the punishment they would face if they disobeyed God.

The first major section of the Old Testament ends with Moses handing over leadership to Joshua. Moses himself had disobeyed God during the time in the wilderness, so—like the others in his generation—he did not set foot in Canaan. Moses went up to Mount Nebo in Moab and looked west across the Jordan River to see the promised land. But that's as far as he got. He died and was buried in Moab, and the people mourned his death for 30 days. And although the Moses chapter of the story had ended, the greatest story was far from over.

Live like people of God's Word!

- Why do you think Moses needed to remind the people how they had come so far?
- How do we keep God's word on our hearts and minds? Why do you think that is important?

Moses passes the torch to Joshua

PICTURING THE STORY

As you watch the story unfold in the video, reflect on these questions:

- How is God at work in this part of the story?
- What part of the story stands out for you? Why?
- What part of the story would you like to know more about?
- What question would you like to ask someone in the story?
- What part of this story seems to connect most with your life?

SINGING AND PRAYING THE STORY

The book of Psalms found in the Bible was the worship book of the people of Israel. The psalms are prayers and songs used to offer praise and thanks to God, ask for God's help, seek God's forgiveness, remember God's actions, and even complain or cry out to God. Christians use the psalms the very same way as we worship and as we reflect on our relationship with God.

Psalm 1
An instructional psalm that praises God's law.
The Hebrew word translated as "law" is *torah*, which can be translated as "teaching" or "instruction." As you read the psalm, think about how important the *torah* was and is in the lives of God's people.

Psalm 105:23-45
A psalm remembering how God led the people out of Egypt and through the wilderness.
How does this psalm connect with the story?

MARK IT

Choose one or more of the following passages from today's section of the story to read during the coming week. Mark your reading using the marking method shown here.

Exodus 3:1-22

Exodus 32:1-35

Leviticus 16:1-34

Deuteronomy 6:1-25

Marking Your Bible

Make notes about the questions and insights you have as you read your Bible. The following symbols might be helpful.

*   A chapter or verse important to me

!   A new idea

√   A passage to memorize

?   Something not clear to me

∞   God's love

℗   A promise from God

≈   Something that connects with my experience

†   My relationship with God

↔   My relationships with others

Next Time

In chapter 4 we will see and hear God's people enter the promised land. We will also see how God appointed leaders called judges to help the people keep the land when peoples from all sides tried to push them out. To help prepare for the next chapter, you are encouraged to read the following pieces from *Lutheran Study Bible*:

- Historical Books Introduction, pages 361-362
- Joshua Introduction, pages 363-364
- Judges Introduction, pages 402-403
- Ruth Introduction, pages 442-443

4

GETTING SETTLED
Joshua–Ruth

Holy land, holy war . . . unsettling times . . . and a love story

Joshua sends spies to Jericho

- In the New Testament, Rahab is described as a person of faith in Hebrews 11:31. In the book of James, she is said to be justified (made right with God) by her works, namely helping the spies (James 2:25). How is faith joined with works in your life?

God leads the people across the Jordan River

- The Israelites put up stones to remember God's hand in helping them cross the Jordan River. What symbols help you remember God's involvement in your life?

JOSHUA, JORDAN, AND JERICHO (Joshua 1–6)
Slavery in Egypt was a distant memory, and the forty years of wilderness wandering were finally at an end. The land that God had promised to Israel's first parents, Abraham and Sarah, was in sight. God told Joshua it was time to cross the Jordan River into the land God was going to give them. Joshua's own name meaning, "the LORD saves," was a reminder that God would lead and protect the people as they entered Canaan.

But moving in wasn't going to be a simple thing. Joshua knew that. Many other people called Canaan home too, so no one already living in Canaan was about to throw the Israelites a welcome-home party. Joshua wisely sent ahead some spies to the nearby city of Jericho. The spy mission might have been a bust, except for the bravery of a local prostitute named Rahab. When local authorities got suspicious, Rahab lied to protect the spies and hid them till dark. The spies made it back to Joshua and gave a glowing report, saying the land was ripe for the picking.

The next challenge was getting all the Israelite people safely across the Jordan River. No time to build big ferry boats. No problem. Remember, God was leading the people. The priests carried the ark of the covenant to the water's edge, and when their feet touched the water, it was like a Red Sea redo. The waters of the Jordan piled up in both directions, and the people walked across the dry river bed. Imagine what the Canaanites were thinking as they watched this happen!

After building a memorial altar as a reminder of the miracle crossing, Joshua and the people moved on to Jericho, their first strategic target. Led by the ark of the covenant and seven priests carrying seven ram horn trumpets, the people walked around the walls of the city seven days in a row. No need for battering rams or tall ladders. On day seven, the people shouted and the walls fell. All the people and animals of Jericho died in the collapse or were killed by the Israelites, except for the prostitute Rahab and her family. They were spared because she had helped the spies, and they lived in Israel for generations after.

Jericho falls

- What do you think of the idea that God takes sides in wars or conflicts?

HOLY WAR (Joshua 7–12)

Jericho was just the beginning. Moving into a land already occupied led to battles and bloodshed, and some bad faith within the ranks. An example of broken faith was an Israelite man named Achan. When the Israelites captured cities in Canaan, some or all of the loot in the city was to be devoted to God, meaning given to God's treasury. Achan swiped some of these things. His bad move not only affected him (he was later stoned to death), but it hurt all of the people. Near the city of Ai, about three dozen Israelites were ambushed and killed. God told Joshua and the people that the deaths were punishment for Israel's sin. Actually, it was Achan's sin, but it affected all the people. They were in it together. All of it. The good and the bad. The idea that the sins and bad faith of one or some affects the lives of all is repeated often in the Old Testament.

The setback at Ai was temporary. God convinced Joshua to regroup and go after Ai. He and the Israelites did as God commanded. It wasn't pretty. Like Jericho, Ai was burned to a heap of ruins and all of its people were killed. Other kings and their territories also were defeated, including a union of kings from northern Canaan. By the time Joshua had completed phase one of the invasion, land he had taken stretched almost all the way back to Goshen in Egypt through the Negeb region, and all the way up to northern Canaan. A whole list of conquered kings is recorded in Joshua 12.

Bloodshed and bad faith

- What do you think of the idea that the sin or broken faith of one or a few can affect the lives—or even the faith—of all? Can you think of an example of this?

Joshua and God's people claim Canaan

- In your opinion, can war ever be holy? Why or why not?
- How do you react to this statement: "Joshua and the people were simply reclaiming the land God had promised to give to their ancestors Abraham and Sarah." In what ways do you see this statement continuing to affect this land today?

- What do you think it would be like to live in a town or city or country where everyone had exactly the same religious beliefs?

A LAND DIVIDED BUT UNSETTLED

(Joshua 13:1—Judges 3:6)

That was that. The land was conquered. Right? Not quite. Much land had been occupied and territories were passed out to the twelve tribes of Israel, but several areas remained unconquered, especially places like Gaza and the land of the Philistines and other sections to the north.

The division of the land into tribal territories is described in detail in the book of Joshua. In addition to the tribal lands, certain cities were set aside for the Levi tribal families. Levi was the tribe assigned to take care of all the priestly duties for the whole nation. So, instead of getting its own geographic territory, this tribe received a share of cities in different regions. Because of this family's special assignment, the other tribes took care of the Levites' needs by providing sacrifices of meat and grain to God. The Levite priests got to keep a portion of the offerings for themselves and their families.

The division of the land also included cities of refuge. These were places a person could run to if he or she accidentally caused the death of an Israelite neighbor. According to Israelite law, the person was to be protected in the refuge city from any relative or friend of the victim who came seeking revenge. The person was due a fair trial before the whole congregation. Yes, that's what it's called in Joshua 20—a congregation. The Israelite people were God's people, so no matter where they lived, they were like a community of faith, a congregation.

*Joshua and the people
promise to serve God*

- Why do you think it is hard to serve God only?

Eventually Joshua grew old and was near death. He gathered all the tribes together one last time, so they could remember the covenant agreements God had made with them and their ancestors. The promised land was a gift from God, as long as the people remembered to worship God alone and live according to God's laws. Joshua warned that they might be tempted to follow other gods, but the people confidently promised to serve God.

After Joshua died, God did not appoint a new leader for the nation. The tribes had to fend for themselves against unfriendly local neighbors. Some were successful and some weren't. As the book of Judges begins, the situation is very unsettled. The people had gone back on their word to Joshua to serve God only. Some worshiped the Canaanite gods called Baals. So the peoples living in the land who had not been conquered by Joshua started to make life very miserable for the Israelites. In fact, Judges 3 reports that God used these nations to test all of Israel.

After Joshua dies, the people worship other gods

- Are you surprised the people of Israel went back on their promise to worship and serve God only? Why or why not?

YOU BE THE JUDGE!

(Judges 3:7—21:25)

Things were looking bad for the people of Israel and for their future in the land of Canaan. They brought the problems on themselves by worshiping other gods. God could have broken off the covenant with them right then and there. But God keeps promises, so God raised up a string of leaders called judges to help the people get through this dark time.

God appoints judges to lead the people

- Imagine what it would be like to live in a time and place as wild and unsettled as Canaan in the time of the judges. What is your reaction to the violence of these times?

The judges were not like court judges; they were more like sheriffs or militia leaders. Because things were chaotic and fighting was breaking out all over, the judges often had to organize the people to do battle.

The judges were both women and men. Deborah joined with Barak to defeat King Jabin of Hazor and his commander Sisera, whose death by tent peg was especially gruesome. Gideon used a small army and some unconventional methods to defeat a larger Midianite army.

Judges are flawed heroes

- Many parts of the Bible are just plain hard to understand. Sometimes it's just best to say, "I don't get it." From what you know about the Bible, what parts are pretty clear to you? What parts are particularly hard to understand?
- What do you think of the idea that God uses people the way they are, not the way they ought to be?

And then there was Samson, the wildest one of all. He made a name for himself killing Philistines. He fell in love with a woman named Delilah. Not a good move. The Philistines convinced her to find out the secret behind Samson's power. Samson couldn't resist Delilah and finally told her the secret. It was his hair. So one night while he slept, she shaved off all of his hair. The Philistines captured Samson and chained him up between two huge pillars in the temple of their god Dagon. Calling on God one last time, Samson received the strength to pull down the whole place on top of himself and all the Philistines.

There are more stories of infighting and intrigue in the book of Judges. One guy named Abimelech tried to set himself as king over all of Israel. He killed seventy of his own brothers in the process. Eventually, Judges reports that God repaid Abimelech for this crime and for his ambition. He died in battle when a woman threw a big rock from a tower and hit him in the head.

Wild and unsettled times

In another story, one of the judges named Jephthah made a silly vow to God. He promised if God would give him victory in battle, he would offer as a sacrifice the first person he saw when he returned home victorious. Imagine his horror when the first one to greet him at home was his young daughter, but he didn't go back on the vow he had made to God. He made good on his promise and sacrificed his daughter to God.

It was a wild and unsettled time in the land. The end of the book of Judges puts it this way: "In those days there was no king in Israel; all the people did what was right in their own eyes."

WHERE YOU GO, I WILL GO (Ruth)

Ruth is a short book of the Bible that is set "in the days when the judges ruled" (Ruth 1:1). It's really a love story, in more ways than one. An Israelite woman named Naomi and her husband moved from Jerusalem to live in the land of Moab. While in Moab, their sons married local Moabite women. One of the daughters-in-law was Ruth. After Naomi's husband and sons died, Naomi decided to move back home to Jerusalem to get help from relatives.

Ruth follows Naomi home

Ruth could have stayed in Moab with her own relatives, but she loved her mother-in-law and decided to return with her to Jerusalem. For us, this may sound like a simple and sensible move, especially for Naomi. But life in that time and place was not simple for women, especially women who had lost their husbands. They had to fend for themselves or rely on the help of relatives to survive. The situation for Ruth was even more complicated. She was a foreign woman, and no one was obligated to help her at all.

Naomi and Ruth came back to Jerusalem at the time of the grain harvest. Fortunately, Israelite law did allow the poor, including a foreigner like Ruth, to pick up any grain left in the field after the harvest. Ruth went to fields owned by a man named Boaz, Naomi's relative on her dead husband's side. Long story short, Boaz noticed Ruth and took care of her and Naomi. In a bold move, he made a deal with a relative who was in line to inherit Naomi's husband's land. Because Ruth was with Naomi, she came along as part of the deal. Boaz married the foreigner Ruth.

Boaz marries Ruth

Here's the really remarkable part of the story. Ruth and Boaz had a son named Obed, who had a son named Jesse. And one of Jesse's sons was David. David, we will discover, would become king of Israel. And more than that, many centuries and generations later, a man named Joseph, descended from the family of King David, would marry a woman named Mary. Their son would be called Jesus (see Matthew 1:1-17).

Ruth, great-grandmother of King David

- Though she was a foreigner, Ruth eventually is named right along with earliest matriarchs and patriarchs of Israel's family. Who do you think of as matriarch or patriarch in your own church or community of faith?
- How have you seen or experienced newcomers and people from other countries shaping your community or your community of faith?

Background Files (Lutheran Study Bible)

Review the timeline on pages 30-32. Notice the approximate time when Joshua leads the invasion of Canaan and when the judges ruled.

Take a look at the map called "Palestine and Key Locations in Joshua and Judges" on pages 2100-2101. Locate some of the places mentioned in the summaries above: Jordan River, Jericho, Ai, land of Philistines, Jerusalem, Moab. Considering that many different peoples already lived in Canaan and the surrounding areas, what strikes you about the tribal territories?

For a quick summary of the judges in Israel, see the chart on page 417.

PICTURING THE STORY

As you watch the story unfold in the video, reflect on these questions:

- As you think about the story of the initial invasion and settlement of Canaan, how would you describe the way God was at work?
- What, if any, questions do these stories raise for you?
- What part of the story would you like to know more about?
- If you could ask any person in these stories a question, who would it be, and what would you ask?
- Do these stories strengthen or test your own faith? If so, how? If not, why not?

SINGING AND PRAYING THE STORY

The book of Psalms found in the Bible was the worship book of the people of Israel. The psalms are prayers and songs used to offer praise and thanks to God, ask for God's help, seek God's forgiveness, remember God's actions, and even complain or cry out to God. Christians use the psalms the very same way as we worship and as we reflect on our relationship with God.

Psalm 47
A psalm that praises God as ruler over the nations.

Many psalms celebrate God's rule over the nations. Here God is also praised for subduing peoples and putting them under the feet of the people of Israel. In what way do you see God as ruling over the nations? How can that be good news? Does it seem strange to praise God for subduing some nations for the sake of others? Why or why not?

Psalm 46

A psalm of trust in God.

This psalm, like many others, expresses the deep faith of one who has turned to God in time of need, especially in a time of trouble. The Israelites would have prayed this psalm in many circumstances. Can you imagine a time when this psalm might be especially meaningful? If so, when? Compare this psalm with Psalm 47. How are they similar? How are the messages of these psalms different?

MARK IT

Choose one or more of the following passages from today's section of the story to read during the coming week. Mark your reading using the marking method shown here.

Joshua 9:1-27   Judges 6:11-40
Judges 16:1-31   Ruth

Marking Your Bible

Make notes about the questions and insights you have as you read your Bible. The following symbols might be helpful.

*   A chapter or verse important to me
!   A new idea
√   A passage to memorize
?   Something not clear to me
∞   God's love
℗   A promise from God
≈   Something that connects with my experience
†   My relationship with God
↔   My relationships with others

Next Time

In chapter 5 we see the settled but divided tribes come together under the rule of a king. For a time the nation is united under one king, but infighting and old tribal rivalries will split the people into two kingdoms. To help prepare for the next chapter, you are encouraged to read the following pieces from *Lutheran Study Bible*:

- Historical Books Introduction, pages 361-362
- 1 Samuel Introduction, pages 449-450
- 2 Samuel Introduction, pages 499-500
- 1 Kings Introduction, pages 543-544
- 2 Kings Introduction, page 592
- 1 Chronicles Introduction, pages 638-639
- 2 Chronicles Introduction, pages 682-683

5

KINGS AND KINGDOMS
Samuel–Chronicles

Israel's tribes unite under one king . . . the temple is built . . . the kingdom splits in two

Hannah dedicates Samuel to God

- What would it be like to dedicate a child to God?
- How are promises made at Baptism like this kind of dedication?

Samuel hears God's call

- How can we hear God's voice?

HERE I AM! (1 Samuel 1–7)

Near the end of the chaotic time marked by the rule of the judges, some new characters enter the story of Israel. One is a brave woman named Hannah. Like her ancestor Sarah, she was not able to have a child, so she went to the holy place at Shiloh and prayed to God for a child. She promised God that if she had a son, she would return him to God. She would make sure he served God.

Hannah's prayers were answered, so she dedicated her son Samuel to God. Her prayer of thanksgiving to God would be echoed centuries later in the prayers of Mary, the mother of Jesus (1 Samuel 2:1-10; Luke 1:46-55). She left Samuel with Eli the priest, who served the holy place at Shiloh.

Eli and his sons were not picture-perfect priests. Far from it. In fact, the sons were downright awful. They cut corners and stole more than their fair share of the offerings to God. They weren't good examples for little Samuel, and their actions threatened all of Israel. Things were so bad that "the word of the LORD was rare . . . visions were not widespread" in the land (1 Samuel 3:1).

Surprising then, that God's voice would be heard at all. But Samuel heard. He didn't know it was God, at first. Old Eli had to help him listen. But when Samuel finally recognized God's voice, he said "Here I am." God was with Samuel and made him a trustworthy priest and prophet. God even made Samuel a judge to lead the people in war against the ever-dangerous Philistines.

TO KING OR NOT TO KING

(1 Samuel 8–15)

As Samuel grew older, he appointed his sons to be judges over Israel, but they took bribes and treated people unfairly. The tribal leaders had reached their limit. It was time for a change, a big change. So they met with Samuel and made a demand: "Give us a king to govern us, like other nations."

Samuel knew that Israel was not like any other nation. The people already had a king—God. God ruled and God led the people. Asking for a human king meant the people didn't trust God. In spite of this, God told Samuel to let the people have what they wanted. God picked out a man named Saul, from the tribe of Benjamin, to be Israel's first king. Samuel made it official by pouring oil over Saul's head. That's called anointing.

At first things went well for Saul. He won victories over some enemies and began to unify the tribes. But he had trouble obeying God. The last straw came when he led Israel in defeating the Amalekites, but did not follow the holy war rule of completely destroying the enemy as a sacrifice to God. God told Samuel that Saul's days were numbered. It was time to anoint a new king.

Israel demands to be ruled by a king

- What makes the appointing of a king such a turning point for the tribes of Israel?

Samuel anoints Saul as Israel's first king

- What would you say is the ideal role of a government leader?
- Do you think faith (not religion) and politics ought to mix? If so, how? If not, why not?

ON A SLING AND A PRAYER

(1 Samuel 16–30)

While Saul was still king, God sent a new candidate for king in Samuel's direction—a son of a shepherd named Jesse from the tribe of Judah. Jesse was the grandson of Ruth, the Moabite. Jesse had several sons, but God's eye was on one of the younger ones—David, to be exact. So, once again, and this time in a much more private ceremony, Samuel anointed Israel's next king. This time it would be David.

It didn't take long before David started to show why God had chosen him. Saul and his army were locked in battle with the Philistines—yes, again. But this time the Philistines had a not-so-secret weapon whose name was Goliath. He was a giant who struck terror into the Israelite army.

Samuel anoints David as Israel's second king

- How would you describe God's role in choosing leaders, especially leaders in communities of faith?

David, the skinny young shepherd, joined Saul's army. Saul had taken a liking to David and made him his armor-bearer. It seems David was a good musician who could calm Saul's nerves with his songs. When no one else would fight Goliath, David volunteered. He tried on Saul's armor, but it was so big for him, he couldn't even walk. So, he dumped the armor and went out to meet Goliath with only a sling and a bag of small stones.

David defeats Goliath

- Can you think of any modern David vs. Goliath stories? What role, if any, does faith play in these stories?

When Goliath saw David, he scoffed at the idea that David could defeat him. David reminded Goliath that he had come in the name and by the power of the God of Israel. Goliath didn't retreat, so David took a stone from his bag, loaded his sling, and whipped it at the giant. Bulls-eye! He hit Goliath in the forehead and killed him. It was the first of many times David would lead Israel in victory over the Philistines and other enemies.

Saul dies in battle

David struck up a friendship with Saul's son Jonathan, but David's relationship with Saul went sour. Saul even tried to kill David a couple of times, but God helped David elude Saul. David had the chance to kill Saul, but spared his life. Eventually, Saul's twenty-year reign ended with his death in battle against—you guessed it—the Philistines.

All Israel chooses David to be king

God promises to establish David's throne forever

- Prophets in Israel would later talk about a messiah who would come from the family of David (Isaiah 11:1-3). Where have you heard the word *messiah* before? What do you think of when you hear the word?

A KING WITH SO MUCH PROMISE (2 Samuel)

Following the death of Saul and Saul's son Jonathan, the process for David taking over as king was begun. Even though Samuel had anointed him king years earlier, the people still had to choose him publicly. He was first anointed king of his own Judah tribe. After some political upheaval and battles, all of Israel chose him to be king. Shortly after that, David brought the ark of the covenant to Jerusalem, beginning a process that ended in making Jerusalem the capital.

David is arguably Israel's greatest king. He is honored as a great warrior and is named as a composer of many psalms. But above all, God honored him by making a covenant with David, a covenant that the prophet Nathan announced to David: "I [God] will establish the throne of your kingdom forever. I will be like a father to him, and he shall be a son to me." In return David promised to build a house, a temple, for God.

David excelled in battle and the borders of the Israelite kingdom were stretched under his rule. But David was also very human. He made some big mistakes. One was his adultery with Bathsheba, the wife of Uriah. David took her and made sure Uriah died in battle. In the midst of this sad situation, Nathan reappeared and this time brought David bad news. Part of God's promise to David would stand, but David's sin would result in sorrow and David would not be allowed to build God's temple.

David's young son with Bathsheba died, and the years that followed were filled with both triumphs and tragedies. His son Absalom died leading a revolt against him. Through it all, God remained faithful to David. David's final words were a psalm of praise and thanksgiving to God (2 Samuel 23:1-6).

One of the last things David did was to buy Araunah's threshing floor, a place where wheat was beaten to harvest the grain. This site in Jerusalem would later become the place where David's son Solomon would build the first temple.

TEMPLE BUILDER (1 Kings 1–11)

David ruled Israel for forty years, the last thirty-three from Jerusalem. As he neared death, a minor dispute arose over who would follow him, but David made it clear that his son Solomon would take over from him. Solomon acted quickly to put down potential opponents and tighten his hold on power. He also followed in his father's footsteps as one who offered sacrifices and prayers of thanks to God.

Solomon pleased God by praying for wisdom in governing the people and in seeing the difference between good and evil. Solomon's wisdom became legendary, and because of this, many wise sayings, or proverbs, in the Bible are credited to Solomon. One of the most famous stories of his wisdom was an episode with two women who both claimed to be the mother of the same child. He suggested that the dispute be settled by cutting the baby in half. One woman agreed to this judgment, but the other refused and told Solomon to give her baby to the other woman. Solomon knew that the second woman, the one who really cared about the child, must be the real mother, and so she was. He gave her the child.

David's sins lead to tragedy

- David was known as one of Israel's greatest leaders and a man of God. He also made some huge mistakes. What might this tell you about those through whom God does great things, including you?

David purchases the site of the future temple

David's son Solomon becomes king

God grants Solomon great wisdom and wealth

- How would you define godly wisdom?

The most important task that defined Solomon's rule was the building of the temple, God's house, in Jerusalem. He worked out a deal with King Hiram of Tyre to get the lumber needed to build the temple. Then Solomon put in place a kind of temple-building draft. He forced thousands of workers from all over the country to go to Lebanon to cut down the cedar trees he had purchased from Hiram, and he made many workers cut huge stones from local quarries. Nearly 500 years from the time the Israelites left Egypt, Solomon began work on the temple in Jerusalem.

Solomon builds the temple

- The temple was said to be God's house, a place where God was present and could be worshiped. How is that similar to or different from our churches? Where is God?

Solomon also built his own stunning palace and made sure the temple was furnished with the most beautiful altar and vessels to use for sacrifices. When the temple was completed, Solomon led a service of dedication. He remembered his father David, and told the people to remember the many ways God had acted to help them in the past. The temple represented God's presence with the people in the land God had promised to give their ancestors.

Solomon turns toward other gods

- What is your reaction to finding out that Solomon worshiped other gods?

Solomon was greater than all the kings of the earth in riches and wisdom. His reign appeared to be the high point in Israel's power. But with such wealth and power come temptations. Like his father, Solomon also made mistakes. He married women from several different nations, and some of them followed their own gods or goddesses. To please his wives he worshiped these other gods, such as Astarte and Milcom. He even built places in the hills near Jerusalem to worship these other gods. As his days neared an end, a man named Jeroboam rebelled against Solomon. This was only a taste of what was to come.

THE GREAT DIVIDE (1 Kings 12:1—16:28)

The death of Solomon turned out to be the death of Israel's united kingdom as well. When Jeroboam couldn't force out Solomon as king, he had to flee to Egypt. When Solomon's son Rehoboam went to Shechem to get the blessing of all Israel as king, Jeroboam and others who were angry showed up at the party. Old rivalries and new tensions (caused by Solomon's policy of drafting workers from the northern tribes) led to what amounted to a civil war, a rebellion against the ruling family of King David. The ten northernmost tribes seceded, forming their own government under the rule of King Jeroboam. The northern kingdom became known as Israel, and its first capital was at Shechem. Rehoboam retreated to Jerusalem, where he became king over the tribes of Judah and Simeon. The southern kingdom's capital was Jerusalem.

Almost immediately Jeroboam set the tone for the stormy history of Israel. He built golden calves at Bethel and Dan, so the people in the north could offer sacrifices close to home rather than go to the temple in Jerusalem. Even though he was warned to tear down these idols, he didn't. God's judgment came down hard on Jeroboam and his family, but the direction of the northern kingdom was set. Rehoboam in the south didn't do much better. He followed the lead of his father Solomon and put up shrines to honor other gods. At one point, the king of Egypt raided Jerusalem and stole some of the treasures of the temple.

In the first decades of the divided kingdom, civil war, political infighting, and idol worship were the name of the game. Some kings tried to restore the worship of God alone, but usually those efforts lasted only a short time. A king named Omri moved the capital of the northern kingdom of Israel to Samaria. Omri "walked in all the way of Jeroboam" and caused Israel to commit terrible sins.

FOUL BAALS (1 Kings 16:29—22:53)

Omri's son Ahab probably was the worst of all the kings "who did evil in the sight of the LORD." He married Jezebel, the daughter of the King of Sidon in Phoenicia, perhaps to form a political alliance. Together, Ahab and Jezebel made a real mess of things. They built an altar to worship the Canaanite god known as Baal and built sacred poles to honor the god known as Asherah. They didn't stop at anything to get what they wanted. In one story, they accused a man named Naboth of cursing Ahab, so they could put him to death and turn Naboth's vineyard into a palace vegetable garden.

An early prophet named Elijah stood up to Ahab and Jezebel and warned them that God would punish them for their evil ways. Elijah also challenged Ahab's prophets of the idol Baal to a showdown. Ahab called the people together to watch. Elijah first rebuilt an altar to Israel's God and put an offering for God on the altar. He told the priests of Baal to do the same.

The united kingdom divides into north and south

- The split in the united kingdom of Israel led to a number of dangerous problems. What do you think some of those problems might have been?

Kings in both north and south turn away from God

- Moses had warned the people over 300 years earlier that they would only be able to keep the land promised to them if they obeyed and worshiped God alone. How do you suppose they forgot this so easily?

Omri moves the northern capital to Samaria

- What "idols" do we turn to?

Ahab and Jezebel—the worst of Israel's rulers

Elijah calls on God to defeat the prophet priests of Baal

- Christians believe in one God, who is creator of all, who chose to bless the people of Israel, who became flesh in Jesus Christ, and who is present as Holy Spirit. What do you think sets God apart from other gods?

- What about people of other religions who believe in other gods? Do you think we should be tolerant of them? Work to destroy them? Try to convert them? Not sure? Why?

Elijah predicts Ahab's death

The priests of Baal called on Baal to consume the offering, but nothing happened. Then Elijah called on God. God sent fire to consume the offering and even the stones of the altar. The amazed crowd followed Elijah's orders to execute the prophet priests of Baal.

Jezebel wasn't happy. She put out a contract on Elijah, who ran away to the wilderness of Mount Horeb to hide out. While there, God spoke to Elijah in a still small voice, telling Elijah to go back and finish the work he had begun. He would anoint a new king to replace Ahab in Israel, and he would anoint a man named Elisha to take his place as prophet in Israel. Eventually Ahab and Jezebel got what they deserved. Elijah predicted that dogs would lick up the blood of Ahab and Jezebel in the same place that dogs had licked the dead body of Naboth. That's exactly what happened. Ahab died in battle and was taken back to Samaria. Dogs licked up the blood that washed onto the ground from his chariot.

Background Files (Lutheran Study Bible)

Review the chart called "Kings of Judah and Israel," page 545. Notice the approximate dates. How many years did the united kingdom last?

Take a look at three maps: "United Kingdom of Israel," "Ancient Jerusalem," and "The Kingdoms of Israel and Judah," pages 2103–2105. Notice how far the kingdoms of David and Solomon expanded. Locate the cities of Jerusalem, Shechem, and Samaria. Compare the size of the Jerusalem under David to its expansion under Solomon.

Find the diagram and illustration of Solomon's temple in Jerusalem, pages 555 and 560. Compare these to the illustration of the tabernacle in the wilderness (page 164). How are the temple and tabernacle similar? How are they different? How do they represent different situations in Israel's history?

PICTURING THE STORY

As you watch the story unfold in the video, reflect on these questions:

- How was God at work in Israel's change from a people without a king to one ruled by a king?
- How was the change to having a king both a positive and a negative for Israel?
- What part of the story would you like to know more about?
- If you could ask any person in these stories a question, who would it be, and what would you ask?
- Faithfulness to God alone is the key theme in these stories. What do you think about this statement? What other themes, if any, do you see?

SINGING AND PRAYING THE STORY

The book of Psalms found in the Bible was the worship book of the people of Israel. The psalms are prayers and songs used to offer praise and thanks to God, ask for God's help, seek God's forgiveness, remember God's actions, and even complain or cry out to God. Christians use the psalms the very same way as we worship and as we reflect on our relationship with God.

Psalm 72

A royal psalm asking for blessings on the king.

Many psalms are called royal psalms because they referred to Israel's kings. Some were used at a coronation (Psalm 2) or a royal wedding (45). Psalm 72 is a prayer of blessing for King Solomon. How does this prayer describe the kind of king Solomon should be? What do you think of this as a model for all who rule in government?

Psalm 101

A royal psalm asking for help to rule with justice and integrity.

Imagine this prayer being prayed by a king who was promising to remain loyal to God alone. What kinds of prayers do we offer for our political leaders?

MARK IT

Choose one or more of the following passages from today's section of the story to read during the coming week. Mark your reading using the marking method shown here.

1 Samuel 2:1-10	2 Samuel 7:1-29
1 Kings 3:1-28	1 Kings 21:1-29

Marking Your Bible

Make notes about the questions and insights you have as you read your Bible. The following symbols might be helpful.

* A chapter or verse important to me
! A new idea
√ A passage to memorize
? Something not clear to me
∞ God's love
℗ A promise from God
≈ Something that connects with my experience
† My relationship with God
↔ My relationships with others

Next Time

In chapter 6 the story of the divided kingdom seems to come to a tragic end. But that is not the end of the story. God leads some of the people back home to start over. To help prepare for the next chapter, you are encouraged to read the following pieces from *Lutheran Study Bible*:

- Historical Books Introduction, pages 361-362
- 2 Kings Introduction, page 592
- 2 Chronicles Introduction, pages 682-683
- Ezra Introduction, pages 736-737
- Nehemiah Introduction, pages 752-753
- Esther Introduction, pages 774-775
- Lamentations Introduction, page 1321
- Daniel Introduction, pages 1421-1422

TRAILS OF TEARS AND JOY

6

2 Kings—Esther, Lamentations, Daniel

Israel falls to Assyria . . . Judah falls to Babylon . . . Into exile and back again

Elisha the prophet and miracle worker anoints Jehu king in Israel

Idol worship continues

- The First Commandment says, "You shall have no other gods." Why do you think it was so hard for the people and their rulers to live out this commandment? What makes it so difficult for us today?

ONE DOWN! (2 Kings 1–17)

The book of 2 Kings continues to tell the stories of the many kings who ruled the northern kingdom (Israel) and the southern kingdom (Judah). The stories echo the viewpoint of the book of Deuteronomy that Israel should worship God alone, and sacrifices to God are to be offered in Jerusalem, the true place of worship.

After Ahab, the string of kings disloyal to God continued. Elisha became the main prophet after Elijah was taken up into heaven in a chariot of fire. Elisha made a name for himself, not only as a prophet but as a miracle worker. He prayed to the LORD and a boy who was dead became alive again. He showed a high commander of the opposing forces of Arameans how to be cured of leprosy, a terrible skin disease. He also anointed a man named Jehu to be king. Jehu tried to erase some of the bad past by tracking down and killing Jezebel and many of Ahab's relatives. He also killed a number of people who worshiped and served the god Baal, but he didn't tear down the golden calf idols built earlier by Jeroboam.

Political infighting and idol worship broke out in the southern kingdom of Judah, too. A young seven-year-old king named Jehoash did fix the parts of the temple that had been destroyed, but he failed to tear down the shrines that had been built to honor other gods. God's judgment against Israel and

Judah mainly came in the form of threats and war with enemies. First, Aram (Syria) to the north threatened. When Hazael of Aram's army surrounded Jerusalem, Judah's King Jehoash had to send all kinds of valuable gifts to buy him off.

Assyria captures the northern kingdom

- How predictable was Israel's bad ending that came in 722 B.C.E.? Why?

Eventually, the powerful army of Assyria invaded the land of Israel and captured Samaria in 722 B.C.E. The Assyrians deported many Israelites to other parts of the Assyrian Empire, and brought people from all the territories they ruled to live in Israel. The northern kingdom (Israel) was gone. The writer of 2 Kings makes it clear that this happened because Israel's leaders and people didn't worship God alone or follow God's commands.

ALL IS LOST (2 Kings 18–25; 2 Chronicles 36:11-21)

During the time that Assyria was close to capturing Samaria in Israel, Assyria also threatened Jerusalem and the southern kingdom of Judah. At this time, Judah was ruled by a king named Hezekiah, who was loyal to God. He destroyed many places of idol worship in the land. He also turned to God when the Assyrian Sennacherib applied great pressure on Jerusalem. When things looked really dark for Jerusalem, an angel of the LORD struck and killed thousands in the Assyrian camp, and Sennacherib's own sons killed him, ending the threat.

King Hezekiah reforms Judah

- How was Hezekiah short-sighted? How do actions in the present affect the future?

This good news was only temporary. About the same time, Hezekiah welcomed visitors from the Babylonian Empire and even showed them the national treasure houses. When asked by the prophet Isaiah what he had shown the Babylonian delegation, Hezekiah said, "Everything." Isaiah's response was sobering: "The days are coming when Babylon will carry off much of this treasure, and your sons [actually great-grandchildren] will be carried off to Babylon." Hezekiah's reply was short-sighted. He said this word from God was good, since it meant there would be peace and security, at least as long as Hezekiah himself lived and ruled.

The book of the law is found in the temple

- Why do you think the discovery of the book of the law was so surprising and so important? Imagine living in a world without laws or rituals. What would it be like?

Hezekiah was followed by Kings Manasseh and Amon, who were both disloyal to God. Manasseh rebuilt some of the altars to foreign gods that Hezekiah had knocked down. In 640 B.C.E., Josiah became king. Josiah reformed the country, based on the book of the law that the high priest Hilkiah found in the temple. Where the book had been is not certain, but when Josiah heard the law read from what may have been portions of Deuteronomy, he tore his clothes in sorrow. He knew that the country probably deserved the judgment God warned would come.

King Josiah tore down most of the altars and shrines to other gods in Judah and killed the priests who served those other gods. He commanded the people to celebrate Passover once again. But Josiah died at the hands of Egyptian King Neco, who was trying to put together an alliance with Assyria against the growing Babylonian threat.

King Josiah reforms Judah

In 597 B.C.E. King Nebuchadnezzar of Babylon captured Jerusalem. He robbed the temple of most of its treasures, just as Isaiah had predicted, and he forced many of Judah's leaders and skilled workers to go into exile in Babylon. Zedekiah was made the puppet king, but he rebelled against Babylon by trying make a treaty with Egypt. Nebuchadnezzar crushed the rebellion and burned down the temple and city walls in 586 B.C.E. Just like Israel before, Judah was now gone.

Babylon defeats Judah and destroys Jerusalem

HOW CAN WE SING THE LORD'S SONG IN A FOREIGN LAND? (Lamentations; Daniel 1–6)

Why had the story turned so bad? For failing to trust in and worship God alone, God's presence departed from the temple and Jerusalem. The enemies of God's people were given the keys to the city. No single book records the history of what happened in Babylon. But this was clearly seen as both a time of punishment and a time of renewal. It was a time to grieve and a time to learn from past mistakes.

The book of Lamentations is a collection of five poems that mourn the destruction of Jerusalem by the Babylonians in 586 B.C.E. These sad prayers, or laments, are credited to the prophet Jeremiah. The words cry out to God, who brought the Babylonians to judge God's people and teach them a painful lesson. Psalm 137 is also a lament prayed by someone who was crying out to God in captivity in Babylon. In this lament you can hear the sorrow, the anger, and the questions: Why God? How long, God?

The exile was a time for grieving and for learning from past mistakes

- God's people cried out to God using prayers of deepest grief called laments. Why do you think this was important? What laments have you cried?

The exile was a time to remain faithful

- How can we support those who face the testing of their faith in God?

The first half of the book of Daniel tells the story of a faithful Israelite named Daniel who was living in the court of Nebuchadnezzar. This story provides a different picture and a slightly different message. Daniel and his friends were asked to turn their backs on God and worship the statue of himself that Nebuchadnezzar had set up. When they refused to do this and remained faithful to God instead, the friends were thrown in a fiery furnace, where God protected them from being burned alive. Daniel was thrown into a den of lions, but God saved him, too. The king was so amazed that he worshiped Daniel's God.

The situation was bad and very sad. But God still was in charge of the future. The message of Daniel was clear: Keep the faith even in this foreign land, because God protects those who remain faithful. Be hopeful that God will lead the people home again.

Persian King Cyrus ends Israel's exile in Babylon

- In the book of Isaiah, Persian King Cyrus is referred to as God's shepherd (44:28). Do you think it is surprising that a non-Israelite is described this way? Why or why not?

GOING HOME (2 Chronicles 36:22-23; Ezra 1–2; Isaiah 40–43)

Just under sixty years had passed since the first group of Israelites living in Judah were forced into exile in Babylon. That's when the Persian Empire, led by new King Cyrus, defeated Babylon. Cyrus believed that a happy empire was a united one. He declared in a written statement that the LORD God had given the kingdoms of the earth and charged him to build God a house in Jerusalem! And God's people living in exile were free to go home to help rebuild the temple and the city.

Imagine the excitement of the Jews in the exiled community. The exile was over and people could go home. But the trip was not an easy one. Miles of difficult desert separated Babylonia and Judah. Some people decided to stay in Babylon and other parts of Persia. Many decided it was worth the risk and headed home. The book of Ezra (chapters 1 and 2) reports that the heads of the families of Judah and Benjamin and many Levites and priests led the returning group, which was also allowed to bring back the temple vessels that Nebuchadnezzar had stolen years before.

The prophet Isaiah had seen this day coming. His beautiful words were filled with promise: Jerusalem had served its term and its penalty was paid. God would make a straight path through the desert for those who wanted to return to Jerusalem (Isaiah 40:1-5). God would be Israel's redeemer. In Hebrew, the word for *redeemer* refers to a relative who buys back a family member who has been forced into slavery. God was redeeming the people of Israel, in the same way God redeemed their ancestors who were enslaved in Egypt.

Many Israelites head home to Judah and Jerusalem

- What do you think of the idea that the exile was God's way of penalizing the people of Israel?
- What, if anything, enslaves you?

RECONSTRUCTION AND RECLAIMED IDENTITY

(Ezra, Nehemiah)

The story of the people's return to Jerusalem and the surrounding area is told in the books of Ezra and Nehemiah. The first order of business was to start worshiping again and offering sacrifices at the old temple site in Jerusalem. Next came the laying of the temple foundation. When the foundation was completed, the people celebrated. But the people of the surrounding land were not happy about the temple being rebuilt. So opposition popped up time and again.

The second temple is constructed in Jerusalem in 515 B.C.E.

During a time of delay in reconstruction, prophets named Haggai and Zechariah encouraged the people to keep at the project. Many people had rebuilt their own private homes, but God's house was still unfinished. Finally, in 515 B.C.E., the second temple in Jerusalem was completed and dedicated.

- What issues or projects are worth completing, no matter what opponents or circumstances arise?

Some years later a Jewish man named Nehemiah was still living in Persia. News came from friends back in Jerusalem that the walls of the city were still in ruins. He worked as the personal wine server for Persian King Artaxerxes. Nehemiah was granted permission to go home and rebuild the city walls. The job was a tough one. Just as local people opposed the rebuilding of the temple, they also tried to stop the rebuilding of the city walls. Once the enemies of the project were dealt with, the building of the three-foot-thick walls was completed in less than two months. It is difficult to say the exact date the wall was completed, but it probably was several years after the temple was reconstructed.

The walls of Jerusalem are rebuilt

- What influences, both inside and outside of our communities of faith, threaten our relationship with God?

The people reclaim their identity as people of God's law

- Ezra and Nehemiah were considered reformers. What do you think needs reform or rebuilding in the church today?

The return to Jerusalem and the rebuilding the temple and city were important steps in returning to true worship of God. Another important step had to do with rebuilding the peoples' lives around the laws and commandments of God. The people were called to live by these laws. To ensure that the people really were true to their identity as God's chosen people, some strict rules were put into effect. For example, the rule of no work on the Sabbath was put in place once again. And Jewish men who were married to foreign wives were told to divorce them. This probably led to some sad breakups and severe conditions for many of the women and children in these families.

Esther becomes queen of Persia

- The Jewish people have often been the target of unjust persecution. What can we do to help those who are treated unjustly, especially those who suffer persecution?

QUEEN IN PERSIA (Esther)

Jerusalem and its temple were being rebuilt, and many Jews went home to Judah to start over. Other Jewish families did not return. Many stayed in the lands where they had been forced to resettle when Assyria and then Babylon conquered the nation. Eventually, the Persian Empire took over these lands and stretched as far east as India and as far west as northern Greece.

Esther is the story of a young Jewish woman living in Persia. Her story takes place in Susa, the capital city of Persia. At the time, Ahasuerus, also known as Xerxes I, was the king of Persia. He ruled from 486 to 465 B.C.E. Esther's story provides one picture of what life may have been like for Jews living outside their homeland. It's an entertaining story full of plot twists and humor, but it's also deadly serious.

The story revolves around the evil plot of Haman, the Persian king's highest official. Haman wanted the king to condemn all the Jewish people of the kingdom to death. This is where Esther saved the day. Without revealing her Jewish heritage, Esther entered the king's empire-wide princess search. She won the heart of King Ahasuerus and was crowned the new queen.

Esther saves her people and Purim is celebrated

- Who would you identify as a hero? Why?

Meanwhile, Esther's uncle Mordecai discovered Haman's plot and secretly worked with Esther to turn the tables on Haman, who ended up being hanged on the same gallows he had built to execute Mordecai. Not only that, Mordecai replaced Haman as the king's highest official. Esther and Mordecai ordered the Jewish people in the land to celebrate a festival called Purim to commemorate the day they were saved. Purim is still celebrated today.

Review the timeline on pages 30-32. Notice how many years are covered by the events in this chapter of Israel's story. Notice also the kingdoms and leaders listed at the bottom of the timeline. How many years passed between the building of the first temple and the rebuilding of the temple after the time of the exile?

Review again the chart of "Kings of Judah and Israel," page 545.

Locate the map of "Jerusalem in Nehemiah's Time," page 755. Use the map to trace his inspection of the walls and his plan to rebuild (see Nehemiah 2:11—3:32).

Review the maps called "Ancient Assyrian Empire," "Ancient Babylonian Empire," and "Ancient Persian Kingdom," pages 2106-2107. Notice the dates that coincide with the exile and return of the people of both Israel and Judah. Knowing these journeys had to be taken by foot, can you see why not all the Jewish people living in distant places chose to go back home? Why do you think these kingdoms and the kingdom of Egypt often invaded and fought to capture the land of Israel?

PICTURING THE STORY

As you watch the story unfold in the video, reflect on these questions:

* How was God at work both in the defeat and exile of Israel and Judah and in the return home?
* What part of the story was most surprising to you? Why?
* What part of the story would you like to know more about?
* If you could ask any person in these stories a question, who would it be, and what would you ask?
* What is the most important theme you hear and see in this part of the story of God's people?

SINGING AND PRAYING THE STORY

The book of Psalms found in the Bible was the worship book of the people of Israel. The psalms are prayers and songs used to offer praise and thanks to God, ask for God's help, seek God's forgiveness, remember God's actions, and even complain or cry out to God. Christians use the psalms the very same way as we worship and as we reflect on our relationship with God.

Psalm 137
A prayer of lament and a cry for help.

Imagine the people praying this prayer while in exile in Babylon. Their captors made fun of their situation and asked the people to sing songs of Zion. Zion was a name for Jerusalem, so being forced to sing songs about their lost home would have been especially painful. In what times do we sing and pray prayers of sorrow?

Psalm 85

A prayer for help and restoration.

This psalm could have been sung and prayed when the people returned home. God had pardoned the sins of the people and restored the land of Jacob, meaning Israel. The people could not save themselves. Rescue must come from God. How is this theme present in our worship?

MARK IT

Choose one or more of the following passages from today's section of the story to read during the coming week. Mark your reading using the marking method shown here.

2 Kings 5:1-19	2 Kings 22:3-20
Ezra 9:5-15	Nehemiah 1:1-11

Marking Your Bible

Make notes about the questions and insights you have as you read your Bible. The following symbols might be helpful.

* *   A chapter or verse important to me
* !   A new idea
* √   A passage to memorize
* ?   Something not clear to me
* ∞   God's love
* Ⓟ   A promise from God
* ≈   Something that connects with my experience
* †   My relationship with God
* ↔   My relationships with others

Next Time

In chapter 7 we will take a look at the story of God's people through the lenses of the Old Testament prophets. The prophets lived and worked during the time of the kings and kingdoms and into the time after the exile. Their messages from God will help us review the key events and themes that have been introduced. To help prepare for the next chapter, you are encouraged to read the following pieces from *Lutheran Study Bible*. It's a long list, so if you can't get to all the reading, focus on the first five items.

* Prophets Introduction, pages 1088-1090
* Isaiah Introduction, pages 1091-1092
* Jeremiah Introduction, pages 1211-1212
* Lamentations Introduction, page 1321
* Ezekiel Introduction, pages 1337-1338
* Daniel Introduction, pages 1421-1422
* Hosea Introduction, pages 1447-1448
* Joel Introduction, page 1467
* Amos Introduction, pages 1476-1477

* Obadiah Introduction, pages 1492-1493
* Jonah Introduction, pages 1496-1497
* Micah Introduction, pages 1502-1503
* Nahum Introduction, pages 1515-1516
* Habakkuk Introduction, pages 1554-1555
* Zephaniah Introduction, pages 1561-1562
* Haggai Introduction, pages 1569-1570
* Zechariah Introduction, pages 1573-1574
* Malachi Introduction, pages 1589-1590

WHEN GOD SPEAKS

The Prophets

God speaks . . . through the prophets . . . to God's people

Prophets speak God's messages

Three Major and twelve Minor Prophets

• Who comes to mind when you think of a modern-day prophet? Why?

Billy Graham
brings a lot of
people to Christ

WHO WERE THE PROPHETS?

Historical clues about when and where Old Testament prophets lived are not always crystal clear, but the story of Israel's history would be incomplete without looking at them and the messages they delivered. In fact, almost one-third of all the pages in English translations of the Bible are devoted to the prophetic books. These books are not organized in chronological order. Instead, the three largest books, known as the Major Prophets, come first. They are Isaiah, Jeremiah, and Ezekiel. They are followed by the twelve Minor Prophets. (Daniel gets special treatment. More about that later.) Rather than following the order of the prophetic books in the Bible, this summary of the prophets and their messages places them in the order that they appear in the story discussed in chapter 6.

The prophets who have books named for them are not the only ones who appear in the Bible. For example, Samuel was a judge and a priest. He anointed Saul and David as Israel's first kings. Nathan functioned as a wise advisor to the king. Elijah and Elisha were early prophets, too. God spoke through them and performed miraculous deeds.

Mainly, the prophets spoke God's messages to the kings, the religious leaders, and the people of Israel and Judah. Sometimes we think of prophets as predictors of the future. But they were much more than that. Their messages brought past, present, and future together. They delivered reminders of God's saving help and commands, making the people examine how they were living in the present. And they delivered warnings about what could and would happen in the future, if the people didn't change their ways.

B.C.E. ± Before the common era (while Christ was living)

- How would you say the future is based on the past and present? How do you see this relating to the message of the prophets?
- If you could get the world to listen to one message from God, what would it be?

780–697 B.C.E.

Amos

- Does it surprise you that the prophets delivered so many messages about justice and caring for the poor? Why or why not?

Hosea

- Another key message the prophets brought was about trust in God. How is trust broken? How do we break trust with God?

Key messages from God delivered by the prophets included these:

- Be faithful to God alone and return to obeying the laws given to Moses.
- Repent for evil actions, especially worshiping other gods and treating the poor unfairly.
- Trust in God and not in political alliances.
- God forgives you and will give you a new start.
- The future is in God's hands.

EARLY WARNING (Amos, Hosea, Isaiah, Micah)

The first group of prophets appeared in the eighth century B.C.E. and spoke their messages between about 775 and 700. The united kingdom had already split into north (Israel) and south (Judah). Elijah and Elisha had done their work as prophets earlier, addressing the situation in the northern kingdom.

Amos was a shepherd and fig tree farmer from Judah. Around 780–750 B.C.E. Amos went north to the royal sanctuary at Bethel and spoke God's messages to King Jeroboam and many of the wealthiest people of Israel. He warned Israel of a coming day of the LORD, meaning a day of judgment. This warning seemed to come to pass when Assyria defeated Israel in 722 B.C.E. Amos' most important message had to do with God's desire for justice. The people of Israel were living well and some even had second homes. But many were getting rich by cheating and mistreating the poor. Amos delivered this message to the people: True faithfulness is trusting in God alone, and treating all neighbors with justice.

Hosea was active as a prophet for a long period during the reign of five different kings in Israel and Judah between 769 and 697 B.C.E. His personal life mirrored his message. As God commanded, he married a prostitute named Gomer. Later, he married another woman who was unfaithful to him. Both marriages symbolized the way Israel and Judah had acted in their relationship with God. They had worshiped the Canaanite fertility gods such as Baal. The leaders had also shown a lack of trust in God by trying to make treaties with nations such as Assyria and Egypt. Hosea pleaded with them to repent and return to God, and warned of punishment and even the coming exile.

Isaiah was a prophet who was active in Judah from about 742 to 700 B.C.E. This was a time when Assyria was threatening and eventually destroyed Samaria, the capital of Israel. The message of Isaiah begins with harsh words of judgment against Judah and its capital city of Jerusalem. The people had abandoned God's ways, followed other gods, and treated the poor unjustly. Isaiah also warned against alliances with foreign powers. Along with warnings of judgment to come, Isaiah delivered God's promise to raise up a messiah-like leader to guide the people. The first portion of Isaiah ends with the story of Isaiah and King Hezekiah, in the days when Sennacherib of Assyria threatened to capture Jerusalem (see Isaiah 36–39).

Isaiah

Micah came from a small village twenty-five miles southwest of Jerusalem. He probably delivered messages from God between about 738 and 700 B.C.E. These were messages of warning and hope to both Israel and Judah. Messages of judgment were usually directed to powerful politicians, priests, and greedy traders who had abandoned God and mistreated the poor. Messages of hope were directed to people without power who remained faithful to God and God's covenant with Israel. Perhaps the most famous saying from the prophet Micah is this: "What does the LORD require of you but to do justice, and to love kindness, and to walk humbly with your God?" (6:8).

Micah

STORM CLOUDS GATHER

(Zephaniah, Jeremiah, Habakkuk, Nahum)
By the time the next set of prophets came on the scene, the northern kingdom of Israel was long gone. The Assyrians had captured Israel and threatened the small southern kingdom of Judah, which now stood alone. The Babylonian Empire was on the rise, and Egypt (to the west of Judah) was always a threat or a potential ally.

640–586 B.C.E.

Zephaniah

Zephaniah preached his messages from God sometime during the reign of King Josiah of Judah, between 640 and 609 B.C.E. He had harsh words for the priests in Judah who allowed the worship of idols, and for officials in Jerusalem who acted unjustly and abandoned faith in God. He also condemned the king's sons for their love of foreign clothes and their crooked deals. He warned of a disastrous Day of the LORD that was coming, when

- It's clear that the prophets believed that politics and religion were supposed to mix. God was the ultimate ruler. How do we translate this kind of message to our own situation, where religion and government are said to be separate?

Judah would feel God's anger. The end of the short book of Zephaniah, however, paints a more promising picture. God will forgive the people, who will rejoice and celebrate their restored fortunes.

Jeremiah

• Do you agree or disagree with this statement: "People don't usually like to hear the truth." Why or why not?

Jeremiah was called by God to be a prophet in Judah in 626 B.C.E. He continued to preach God's messages until he died in 586 B.C.E., the year Babylon destroyed the temple in Jerusalem and tore down the city's walls. Jeremiah's messages addressed the problem of lack of faith. After King Josiah died, Judah's kings turned to foreign powers for help, instead of trusting in God. They turned first to Egypt. But then the Babylonians defeated Egypt and Assyria, and Judah came under Babylonian control. Jeremiah's messages talked of disaster and uncertainty. His messages about Judah's unfaithfulness angered his friends and neighbors who thought Jerusalem would never be defeated. After Jerusalem was captured and people were taken away to exile in Babylon, Jeremiah also sent messages of hope and the promise of a new covenant to come.

Habakkuk

Habakkuk was a prophet living in Judah around 600 B.C.E. Habakkuk not only brought God's message, he complained to God about the situation in Judah. The little country was feeling the pinch of the superpower Babylon. As the danger from outside increased, Habakkuk complained that corruption in the city of Jerusalem was increasing. God would bring disaster on idol worshipers and the arrogant ones who trusted in wealth. Habakkuk prayed for the people, even though he knew disaster was sure to come. And he continued to trust in God, even though times were as bad as they could get.

Nahum

• What do you think about the idea of celebrating the destruction of an enemy?

Nahum preached his message in Judah around 612 B.C.E. His message spoke to the political uncertainty of the day as well. It was mainly a message of judgment directed toward Nineveh, the capital of the mighty Assyrian Empire. Assyria was known for the brutal way it defeated people and treated those who were conquered. Nahum announced the coming destruction of Nineveh, and called the people of Judah to celebrate. His message: God is a divine warrior who holds oppressive nations accountable for their evil acts, and sets oppressed people free.

HOPE RESTORED

(Ezekiel, Isaiah II, Haggai, Zechariah)

In spite of some kings who tried to reform the nation of Judah, too much corruption and bad faith were alive and well in Jerusalem. Ezekiel summarized the situation by saying that things were so bad that God's presence had left the temple in Jerusalem. Judah was defeated and sent into exile. During this dark time the prophets, including Ezekiel, brought messages of hope and restoration.

593–515 B.C.E.

Ezekiel served as a prophet from 593 B.C.E., before the final destruction of Jerusalem, to 571 B.C.E. While living among the first wave of exiles in Babylon, he had some powerful visions about the coming destruction of Jerusalem. He described how the priests allowed worship of idols right in the temple area. He accused the priests and predicted their destruction. He also condemned those who gave false hope to the people. God would abandon Jerusalem to destruction. But Ezekiel also preached hopeful visions. He described how God's people were like dry skeleton bones in exile, but God would breathe new life into those bones and make them walk. Ezekiel envisioned a new temple in Jerusalem, as well as God's return.

Ezekiel

- Some people talked about how beautiful Ezekiel's words were, but they didn't take his words to heart and act on them. How do we hear God's words and take them to heart?

Isaiah II was an unknown prophet whose message is found primarily in Isaiah 40–56. He spoke to the people living in exile in Babylon sometime between 586 and 540 B.C.E. His words are some of the most beautiful and most quoted passages in the Bible. He spoke of God forgiving the people of their sins and ending their time of punishment in Babylon. God would lead the people home to rebuild Jerusalem, and nations would be drawn to worship God. Isaiah 40–56 also includes a number of passages called *Servant Songs*. These passages describe a servant who was punished for the sins of the people. After Jesus died and rose, these Servant Songs were often used to describe what Jesus had done to save humanity from sin.

Isaiah II

- What words of God give you hope?

Haggai brought his message from God during a six-month period in 520 B.C.E. Cyrus of Persia wrote a decree allowing the Jewish people to leave Babylon in 539 B.C.E. and return home. Haggai spoke to the people who returned to Jerusalem. The building of the temple foundation had begun, but work had slowed as people took care of their own housing needs. Haggai's message was focused on rebuilding the temple. Only when the temple was rebuilt would God be fully present with the people, Haggai said.

Haggai

A rebuilt temple meant a restored community, and a restored identity as God's people in the world.

Zechariah

• How might we share our vision of worshiping God with those who don't believe in our God?

Zechariah also began his prophetic preaching in 520 B.C.E. Like Haggai, he brought messages about a renewed community of faith in Jerusalem. In a series of visions, he described a restored temple in Jerusalem as the center of the world. He envisioned priests rededicated to serving God and leading the people in proper worship. The second part of the book of Zechariah begins with chapter 9. It is uncertain whether these messages were written later, or whether they were written by another prophet in Zechariah's name. In any case, New Testament writers drew on images from this part of Zechariah. The image of the triumphant king riding into Zion or Jerusalem (Zechariah 9:9) is compared to Jesus entering Jerusalem before the events leading to his death (Matthew 21:5). The book of Revelation (22:1-3) shares Zechariah's vision of God's victory over all enemies (Zechariah 14:8-11).

450–165 B.C.E.

Obadiah

IT'S GOD'S FUTURE (Obadiah, Joel, Malachi, Daniel)
Jerusalem was resettled and the second temple had been built. But the people of Judah continued to be under the control of larger empires.

Obadiah preached his message some time after Jerusalem was destroyed, but the year is uncertain. Obadiah's short message was a message of judgment against Judah's neighboring country, Edom. Edom was understood to be Israel's "brother." In the Old Testament, the roots of the people of Edom are traced back to Esau, the twin brother of Jacob (later renamed Israel). Apparently the people of Edom rejoiced in the destruction of Jerusalem, and took part in looting the city as it was being destroyed. For their actions, God would punish Edom. The end of the prophecy envisions the restoration of Zion (Jerusalem).

Joel

• How does a description of God as judge seem to fit with Joel's description of God as gracious, loving, and slow to anger? How have you experienced both sides of God?

Joel received his message from God sometime after the return from exile and before 348 B.C.E., the year the city of Tyre in Phoenicia was destroyed. Joel spoke of God sending an army of locusts on the land as punishment for sin. The locust army and the destruction it would bring were a call to return to God and worship God alone. If the people would return, Joel said, God "is gracious and merciful, slow to anger, and abounding in steadfast love" (2:13). Joel's message envisioned Jerusalem being restored and God's spirit being poured out on all people (2:29). God and the people would live in Judah and Jerusalem for all generations.

Malachi preached his message in Judah sometime after the return from the exile, but the exact date is hard to pinpoint. The temple and Jerusalem itself had been rebuilt, but life was still very hard for the Jewish people. The priests were offering improper sacrifices, and the people were not providing a fair share of offerings. Worshiping other gods and oppressing people who were poor and needy, including widows and orphans, were problems once again. Malachi envisioned a great day of the LORD coming, when those who were unfaithful would be destroyed. For those who respected and worshiped God properly, "the sun of righteousness shall rise, with healing in its wings" (4:2).

Daniel is listed among the prophets in our modern Christian versions of the Old Testament. But in the original Hebrew Scriptures, Daniel appears in a section called the Writings. As seen in the previous chapter, the book's first six chapters tell the story of Daniel and his friends living in Babylon. The second half of the book provides a series of visions that are unlike most of the other books of prophecy. This kind of literature is called *apocalyptic*. That's literature filled with unusual images, including one called the Antichrist, and focusing on the end times when God will battle evil. Daniel's visions include political references that stretch from the time of the Babylonian exile all the way to the centuries after Alexander the Great, who died in 323 B.C.E. The message is clear: evil will not have the last word. God's people live in a chaotic and violent world, but God is in charge. God will raise the faithful from the dead to everlasting life (12:2-4).

Malachi

• Do you think there is a proper way to live out your faith? If not, why not? If so, what does this look like?

Daniel

• Daniel's visions have been linked to the apocalyptic visions in Revelation in the New Testament. Some interpret these visions as predictions of current world events. What do you think about this? Do you think Daniel was meant to be read this way?

GOD'S SURPRISING GRACE
(Jonah)

Jonah is not like any other prophetic book in the Bible. The prophetic speech or sermon in the book is only one verse long. The rest of the book tells the story of the prophet Jonah, who was called by God to take a message to Nineveh, the capital city of the Assyrian Empire. Nineveh was destroyed in 612 B.C.E., when the Babylonians defeated Assyria. On that basis, it may seem as if Jonah lived in the time after the hated Assyrians had defeated Israel in 722 B.C.E., and before 612 B.C.E. because, in the story,

612–? B.C.E.

Jonah

• What do you know or remember about the story of Jonah? Why didn't Jonah want to go to Nineveh and deliver God's message? (If you aren't sure, read the story. It's short.)

Nineveh is not yet destroyed. But many think the book comes from a much later time, even after the people returned from the exile.

The story of Jonah is a masterpiece, filled with great plot twists and irony. You might already know the part about Jonah being swallowed by a whale. But the story really is about God and what God does. Read the story with that in mind. Another idea is to read Jonah alongside the short book of the prophet Nahum. Nahum's prophecy calls the people of Israel to rejoice that God will make sure their enemy Nineveh is destroyed. The story of Jonah shows another side. God forgives the people of Nineveh when they repent of their evil ways. The story of Jonah is another reminder to the people of Israel, and to us, that God acts as both judge and savior.

Background Files (Lutheran Study Bible)

Review the timeline on pages 30-32. Notice where the prophets are placed on the timeline. Some prophetic books seem to come from different time periods and so might have multiple authors. Can you see which prophetic books may fit this description?

Review the chart of "Prophets," page 1089. Daniel is listed with the Major Prophets, but only because Daniel is not considered part of the "Twelve," the Minor Prophets. We list Daniel among the prophetic books in our English translation Bibles. But in the original Hebrew Scriptures, Daniel was listed as part of the Writings, and not as a prophetic book.

See the illustration of the Cyrus Cylinder on page 1158. It's one example of how historical artifacts can provide background that helps make the Bible's story clearer. Review why Cyrus was such an important part of the story.

Take a look at the diagram that pictures Ezekiel's vision of the new temple in Jerusalem (page 1404). Read Ezekiel 40–48 if you want a detailed description of the temple and surrounding area.

PICTURING THE STORY

As you watch the story unfold in the video, reflect on these questions:

- Why did God call prophets to speak to the people?
- How well did the leaders and the people listen to the prophets? Why?
- How do the prophets fit in the story of God's people?
- What prophet would you like to know more about? What question would you like to ask that prophet?
- What is the key thing you take away from this short introduction to the prophets in the Bible?

SINGING AND PRAYING THE STORY

The book of Psalms found in the Bible was the worship book of the people of Israel. The psalms are prayers and songs used to offer praise and thanks to God, ask for God's help, seek God's forgiveness, remember God's actions, and even complain or cry out to God. Christians use the psalms the very same way as we worship and as we reflect on our relationship with God.

Psalm 14
An instructional psalm.
How does this psalm echo a key theme of the prophets?

Psalm 68:1-20
A psalm of thanksgiving.
How is God described in this psalm? What themes in this psalm are part of the message of the prophets?

MARK IT

Choose one or more of the following passages from today's section of the story to read during the coming week. Mark your reading using the marking method shown here.

Amos 5:14-24   Jeremiah 31:31-34
Joel 2:23-32   Jonah

Marking Your Bible

Make notes about the questions and insights you have as you read your Bible. The following symbols might be helpful.

* A chapter or verse important to me
! A new idea
√ A passage to memorize
? Something not clear to me
∞ God's love
Ⓟ A promise from God
≈ Something that connects with my experience
† My relationship with God
↔ My relationships with others

Next Time

In chapter 8 we will explore the final group of books in the Old Testament. We will call them Wisdom and Poetry books, but they are also known as the Writings. They help fill in the story of God's people by giving us a clearer picture of how people thought about God and how to live as God's people in the world. To help you prepare for the next chapter, you are encouraged to read the following pieces from *Lutheran Study Bible*.

- Wisdom and Poetry Books Introduction, pages 786-787
- Job Introduction, pages 788-790
- Psalms Introduction, pages 847-848
- Proverbs Introduction, pages 1011-1012
- Ecclesiastes Introduction, pages 1061-1062
- Song of Solomon Introduction, pages 1075-1076

FOR EVERY MATTER UNDER HEAVEN

Wisdom and Poetry Books

Poetry and songs, proverbs and prayers . . . for worship . . . for all of life

Job was a good man who lost everything

- Can you think of examples of bad things happening to good people? How do you or others deal with "why" this suffering happens?

WHY DO THE INNOCENT SUFFER? (Job)

We all experience suffering of one kind or another. It's part of being human. Sometimes suffering touches us directly, and sometimes we see it from a distance. We watch as people face natural disasters such as earthquakes and floods. We see the turmoil and horrible consequences of war and other acts of violence. We see people suffer from hunger or disease. The causes of some kinds of suffering are easy to see, but sometimes suffering comes without explanation. And the questions begin: Why? How long?

The book of Job (rhymes with "robe") is about suffering and its causes. The book is named for the main character (besides God) in the book, who even dared to ask what role God may play in suffering. We would call Job a good guy, a real solid citizen. The Bible calls him "blameless and upright, one who feared God" (1:1). That means he respected God. But suffering hit Job hard. Everything he had was destroyed: his wealth, his health, and his beloved children.

The story says that God allowed a character named Satan to test Job with this suffering to see how he would react. That's a challenging scene that we might struggle to understand. But the book is most interested in what happens when suffering hits. How did Job deal with the suffering? Who helped him deal with it? And where was God?

Friends came to be with Job in his suffering, and they offered various explanations. One of the main explanations was this one: "Job, you must have done something wrong. You are just getting what you deserve." The Bible contains many examples of people thinking this way about suffering, especially in the Old Testament. Job's friends explained that his suffering was punishment for his bad actions, because God punishes those who sin and do evil. Those who live good lives are rewarded with health and wealth and long life. But Job didn't know what he had done wrong, so this explanation didn't help him much. It probably doesn't help us much, either. We can see bad things happen to good people all the time. And some bad characters seem to do pretty well for themselves.

Suffering cannot always be explained

• What do you think is the best way to help someone who is suffering? What can be said? What kinds of things might you choose not to say?

Job prays in the midst of suffering

• How can times of suffering be times of deeper connections with God and others? How have you experienced this?

Job's friends tried other explanations as well, but in the end even God didn't directly answer the question about suffering. Sometimes suffering is a mystery. The book of Job does have important things to say, however, about suffering, about God, and about the world:

• Suffering isn't always a result of sin. Sin and evil do cause suffering, but not all suffering.
• Prayer is a proper response to suffering. This includes prayers of lament, honest cries of anger and anguish to God. Job is commended for talking directly to God.
• God cares for creation and takes delight in it. God invites us to see and delight in the world, too.
• God is with us in all of the ups and downs of life. God is present in our suffering.

The book of Job is not the last word on suffering in the Bible. The New Testament Gospel stories (chapters 10 and 11) proclaim that God loves the world and entered into the suffering of the world through the cross of Jesus Christ.

SONGS FOR ALL TIMES (Psalms)

The book of Psalms contains one hundred fifty prayers, songs, liturgies, and poems used in worship and to mark other occasions, such as the coronation of a king. They were written by many unidentified authors. (Some of the psalms have a superscription such as "of David" or "of Asaph." These terms do not mean David or Asaph wrote these psalms, just that the poem or song is associated with them in some manner.)

The psalms were written for a wide variety of purposes. Some were written primarily for personal use and others for community use. Some help tell the story of the people of Israel. Historical events are remembered and described in some of the psalms. But we also get an up close and personal look into the lives of God's people. In the psalms we see people praising God in times of joy and celebration. We also see people praying in times of suffering and distress. We see them praise God's law and wisdom, and we hear them confess their sins, asking God for forgiveness.

The psalms explore highs and lows in the life of faith. They sing with joy and trust from the mountaintop moments and cry out with pain "out of the depths" (130:1). The psalms weep with those who suffer, laugh with those who celebrate, and teach us all about the long journey of faith.

Psalms is the prayer book of God's people

- How can prayers written so long ago still speak to us and help us speak to God?

Psalms explore the highs and lows of the life of faith

- What part does prayer play in your life?

WOMAN WISDOM CALLS
(Proverbs)

The book of Proverbs is a collection of wise sayings that reflect an understanding of how life is to be lived in relation to God and to neighbors. In this way, the wisdom sayings of Proverbs are related to God's laws and commandments. The beginning of knowledge or wisdom, says Proverbs, is "the fear of the LORD" (1:7). This phrase means respecting and honoring God and living according to God's commands.

Proverbs reflect God's wisdom and law

- How does God's wisdom become our wisdom?

Proverbs reflect life as we know it

- Who is the wisest person you know? What makes that person wise?
- Why do you think wise sayings alone can't make a person right with God?

So, true wisdom comes from listening to God's instruction and living according to it. Wisdom also appears as a woman calling out to people in the street (1:20; 8:1-4), inviting them to her banquet (9:1-6). Wisdom has been with God since the very beginning of time (8:22). The proverbs read like examples of timeless truth, but some may seem more timeless to our ears than others. We can hear the timeless truth in this proverb: "A soft answer turns away wrath, but a harsh word stirs up anger" (15:1). But "The eye that mocks a father . . . will be pecked out by the ravens of the valley" (30:17) may not be a truth we will hear or repeat often today. Mocking a parent is not a good thing, but we don't expect it to bring on some kind of bird attack.

There are many different types of proverbs. The best way to see the difference is to read a few of the different kinds. For example, compare these proverbs:

- 10:1
- 22:6
- 25:11
- 30:29-31

As Christian readers of the Bible, we read the wise sayings of Proverbs with our eyes also on Jesus, who the apostle Paul says, "became for us wisdom from God" (1 Corinthians 1:30). We know that living according to wise sayings cannot make us right with God. Rather, we are made right by God's grace through faith in Christ Jesus.

Ecclesiastes is the memoir of the unknown Teacher

SEARCH FOR MEANING (Ecclesiastes)

The book of Ecclesiastes is written as a kind of personal diary or memoir by someone identified as "the Teacher." Traditionally, the Teacher has been identified as Solomon, the wisest of Israel's kings (1:1). But it is more likely that Ecclesiastes was written much later, perhaps only three or four hundred years before the birth of Jesus.

Ecclesiastes is read by the Jewish community during the Feast of Sukkoth, also called the Feast of Booths, or Ingathering. That festival occurs in the fall of the year and celebrates God's care for the people of Israel as they wandered in the wilderness. The festival also celebrates God's care for life today and the joy that can be found in life, even when life is fragile and unpredictable.

Some see Ecclesiastes as cynical and depressing, reflecting a crisis of faith. But Ecclesiastes can be seen as uplifting. The book helps us understand that realism and skepticism are important parts of faith. The Teacher concludes that once people discover that they cannot find meaning on their own, then they can leave such matters to God and learn to find pleasure in the simple living of life.

The book contains a number of wise sayings, or proverbs. It features these beautiful words that sum up life: "For everything there is a season, and a time for every matter under heaven: a time to be born, and a time to die . . . ." Read the whole list in Ecclesiastes 3:1-8. Other themes in this book include:

- Becoming rich or smart or having fun all the time does not lead to a meaningful life.
- We are all going to die, so no one is finally better than anyone else.
- The world is not fair. The good aren't always rewarded, and the bad do not always get punished.
- We should all find time to enjoy the work and life God has given us.

Ecclesiastes is read during the Jewish festival of Sukkoth

- Do you agree that life can sometimes seem meaningless? How does a person deal with those kinds of feelings?

Enjoy the life God gives

- What do you think of the idea of leaving hard questions and matters to God, and finding pleasure in living life?
- If you could ask the Teacher a question, what would it be?

SET ME AS A SEAL UPON YOUR HEART (Song of Solomon)

The Song of Solomon is a series of love poems between two lovers. The author of the book is unknown, even though it is named for Israel's King Solomon. It was probably written in the third or fourth century B.C.E., some six hundred years after Solomon lived. The book's strong female character and voice suggest that the author may have been a woman.

Song of Solomon is a series of love poems

- Are you surprised that a book of the Bible is a series of poems about human love? Why or why not?

- What makes human love so powerful?
- How is human love like God's love? How do you think it is different?

Like the book of Esther, Song of Solomon is unusual in the Old Testament in that it never mentions God or religious practices. It simply reflects on the beauty and power of human love in all its dimensions. It affirms the goodness of creation, human bodies, and sexuality. Song of Solomon acknowledges that relationships cannot be built only on mutual attraction. They must also include conversation, commitment, faithfulness, and respect. The book claims that love is as strong as death (8:6) and precious beyond all wealth.

Some interpreters of this book saw its love poems as symbolic of the love between God and God's people. The claims about human love take on deeper, fuller meanings when applied to God's love for us. Song of Solomon can be read as a celebration of both human and divine love.

Background Files (Lutheran Study Bible)

Review the chart "Types of Psalms" on pages 849-850. When you have time, read an example or two from each category. How are psalms used in your community of faith? How can you use psalms in your prayer life?

Review the chart "Types of Proverbs" on page 1018. Take time to look at the different examples and explanations. Search Proverbs to find other examples for each of the categories.

PICTURING THE STORY

As you watch the story unfold in the video, reflect on these questions:

- What new things have you learned about suffering, love, and the meaning in life?
- How can the book of Psalms be your prayer book?
- What wisdom do you need? Where can you find it?
- Which of the books mentioned today do you want to get to know more deeply? Why?
- What idea or theme stands out to you in this part of the greatest story?
- Did anything in this video surprise you? If so, what?

SINGING AND PRAYING THE STORY

The book of Psalms found in the Bible was the worship book of the people of Israel. The psalms are prayers and songs used to offer praise and thanks to God, ask for God's help, seek God's forgiveness, remember God's actions, and even complain or cry out to God. Christians use the psalms the very same way as we worship and as we reflect on our relationship with God.

Psalm 23

A psalm expressing trust in God.

Think about when and where you may have heard this psalm before. Why do you think so many people consider it a favorite?

Psalm 13

A psalm crying out to God for help.

Imagine Job praying this prayer of distress. Notice how the psalm begins and ends. What do you see? When in your life would this psalm have reflected your prayer, your conversation with God?

MARK IT

Choose one or more of the following passages from today's section of the story to read during the coming week. Mark your reading using the marking method shown here.

Job 19	Ecclesiastes 3:1-8
Proverbs 22:1-16	Song of Solomon 2:6-17

Marking Your Bible

Make notes about the questions and insights you have as you read your Bible. The following symbols might be helpful.

* ∗   A chapter or verse important to me
* !   A new idea
* √   A passage to memorize
* ?   Something not clear to me
* ∞   God's love
* ℗   A promise from God
* ≈   Something that connects with my experience
* †   My relationship with God
* ↔   My relationships with others

Next Time

In chapter 9 we will review some of the key themes in the Old Testament part of the greatest story. We will also explore how the Old and New Testaments look back and look ahead to help us see the whole story and what it means for our lives. To help you prepare for the next chapter, you are encouraged to read the following pieces from *Lutheran Study Bible*.

* Old Testament Overview, pages 41-43
* Introduction to the Bible, "The Shape of the Sacred Bible," pages 26-27
* "Lutheran Insights that Open the Bible," pages 1538-1543

PEODLE OF PROMISE
The Old Testament Story for Us

9

Ancient promises speak in new ways for a new day

CREATED AND BLESSED

We are part of a big story. As stories go, it is very old. The story the Bible tells stretches all the way back to the beginning of time. It's an old story, but it's also timeless. It's new every day, because God isn't done creating. The story that began long ago and got recorded in ancient stories we call the Old Testament is not finished. It hasn't ended, because it is still being written and told in us!

The story of faith is still being told

- How can the story of faith be both old and new at the same time?

ongoing

Light for all the nations

- Describe a person or people who have been a "light" in your life, or light for the world.

The story of faith told in the Bible is our story. God promised our ancient relatives Abraham and Sarah that their family would be a great nation. And they believed God (Genesis 15:1-6). God also promised to bless this family, so that they could be a blessing to the whole world. The prophet Isaiah speaks of a servant to raise up the tribes of Jacob. That's Abraham and Sarah's family. God will give this servant "as a light to the nations, that my [God's] salvation may reach to the end of the earth" (Isaiah 49:6).

From God's family of faith came the one who said this about himself: "I am the light of the world" (John 8:12). The name of the person who said that is Jesus. For Christians, Jesus is the main character in the story of faith. But the story of God's relationship with the world and with us didn't start with Jesus. It began with his relatives. That's why the whole Bible is our book of faith.

God continues to create and bless

- For what blessings are you especially grateful? What blessings are you willing to share?

We worship the same God who created everything and continues to give us food and fill us with good things (Psalm 104:24-30). Our blessings come from the hand of the same God who blessed Abraham and Sarah and their descendants. We raise our hands to worship God, and we reach out our hands to receive God's blessings. And we use our hands to pass those blessings on to others. That's how the story keeps going.

CALLED AND CLAIMED

The Bible is filled with stories about people who received a call from God. Imagine what that would be like. The phone rings and you hear a voice, or see a text message: "Hi, it's God!" How do you respond to a message like that? The amazing thing is, many did respond. Abraham, Sarah, Jacob, Joseph, Moses, Miriam, Hannah, Deborah, Samuel, Isaiah, Esther. You've heard their stories. Why did they answer? They trusted God's words: "I am the LORD your God . . ." (Exodus 20:1-3). God, "your God." God was there for them.

Hello . . . God calling!

- What message do you wish God would give you? How are you listening?

God is still there—calling and standing by. Psalm 139 reminds just how close God is. God knows us inside and out. God knows when we sit down and when we rise up, even before we start talking, God knows what we are going to say. We can try to get away from God, like Jonah did, but God will find us. We might even try to hide out in the darkness, but it doesn't matter. Darkness is like light to God. Just like God told the people of Israel, "I am your God," God claims us.

We are God's holy people

- How do you feel about God knowing you so well?
- What do you think about being called a holy priest, or being part of the priesthood of all believers?

That God knows us and calls us family is good news—at least most of the time. Sometimes we don't act like family. We make it a habit to mess around with our relationship with God. We act like we can't believe that we are really part of the promise God made to the people of Israel: "You shall be for me a priestly kingdom and a holy nation" (Exodus 19:6). Not only are we family, we serve God as holy priests. We are holy people with a holy purpose. Martin Luther said that baptized Christians are the priesthood of all believers. We share the work of worshiping God, serving our neighbors, and caring for creation.

LOVED AND CHALLENGED

God's holy purpose gets worked out in a word—love. It's a familiar word. Maybe even an overused word. But it's a good word. The Bible is a love story. Sure, there are lots of other words in the Bible, too. Words of destruction and despair and judgment. And God speaks some of those too. But it starts with love. It's a love that is "established forever," just like God's "faithfulness is as firm as the heavens" (Psalm 89:1-2).

Love comes in many forms. There's romantic love, love between friends, and love shared in families. The Bible speaks about all of these. But love for God is most often described in a two-part relationship—our love for God and our love for our neighbors. Love for God is related to the promise of the First Commandment: "The LORD is our God the LORD alone." We are to love God with our whole heart, soul, and might. (Deuteronomy 6:4-9). Loving God with our whole being. How do we do that? There's no simple answer. We can't love God perfectly all the time. We know that for certain. And loving our earthly neighbors can be a real challenge.

Still, that's what God calls us to do in the Bible. God wants love to have a real face and hands. That's God's whole purpose for choosing and blessing people. "You shall love your neighbor as yourself," God says (Leviticus 19:18). God's love is made real through us. The prophet Micah summarizes this so clearly: "What does the LORD require of you but to do justice, and to love kindness, and to walk humbly with your God?" (Micah 6:8). Imagine a world where everyone lived according to this vision! God does.

But God does more than lay out the vision. God also gives us the power to do what God envisions. And when we fall short, God shows the mercy side of love. The people of Israel experienced that mercy over and over when they fell away. As Christians, the mercy of God is made real for us in the grace and forgiveness of Jesus, God's own Son.

It starts with love

Love God and love your neighbor

- How does love start with God?

unconditional

The mercy side of love

- How are we doing, living out God's vision of love?

Looking forward and looking back

- How are the past and the future linked in both the Old and New Testaments?

The promise of Messiah

- Why do you think the promise of a messiah is such a powerful promise?

The Messiah's purpose

- How would you describe your purpose in life? What would your "purpose statement" be?

REMEMBER THE FUTURE

The Old Testament is an important part of the greatest story, but the story doesn't end there. This first part of the Bible looks ahead to the next part, what Christians call the New Testament. But what does it really mean that the Old Testament looks ahead to the New Testament? We actually get a hint from how the New Testament looks back to the Old. The most important example of this revolves around the promise of a coming Messiah. *Messiah* comes from a Hebrew word that means "chosen one" or "anointed one."

In various places in the Old Testament, the Hebrew Scriptures, a coming messiah is described. Sometimes the messiah is actually named. For example, Cyrus of Persia is called a messiah, or chosen one, because God appointed him to defeat the Babylonians and to issue a decree letting the people of Israel leave their captivity in Babylon and go home (see Isaiah 44:28—45:3). Sometimes the people of Israel are called God's "chosen ones," to carry out God's plans and purposes (see Isaiah 42:1-4; 49:1-6).

Often the chosen one is an unnamed individual who God calls to carry out God's vision for peace and justice in the world. This ideal ruler or messiah was to come from the family of David. The prophet Isaiah speaks of a child "born for us, a son given to us" who will be named "Wonderful Counselor, Mighty God, Everlasting Father, Prince of Peace" (Isaiah 9:6-7). It is also the prophet Isaiah who describes a servant who suffers for the sake of the people and even bears their sins (Isaiah 52:13—53:12). It's no wonder that the followers of Jesus who knew the ancient Hebrew Scriptures saw Jesus as the servant who fulfilled the words of the prophets. The Gospel of Matthew looks back to the Hebrew Scriptures several times to makes sense of the life of Jesus, the Messiah. For example, see Matthew 1:22-23. Jesus was the son of Joseph, a descendant of King David, the son of Jesse (see Micah 5:2-5; Matthew 1:1-17).

Jesus himself looked back to the Hebrew Scriptures to describe his mission in the world. One day while teaching in a synagogue (Luke 4:16-22), Jesus read from the scroll of the prophet Isaiah (61:1-2). God chose him for this purpose, he said, "to bring good news to the oppressed, to bind up the brokenhearted, to proclaim liberty to the captives, and release to the prisoners . . . to comfort all who mourn." It's an incredible story. There's never been another story quite like it. And it's our story. We are part of it.

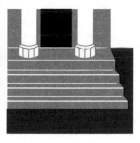

THE TIME BETWEEN THE TESTAMENTS

The Jewish people returned to Judah starting in 539 B.C.E. The new temple was built and dedicated in Jerusalem in 515 B.C.E. Jesus was born about 4 B.C.E. The Bible does not say a great deal about the many years in between these major events. Some books of the Old Testament probably were written during this period. We've said that Daniel may have been written as late as about 164 B.C.E.

We do know that the Jewish people were ruled by a series of powerful outside nations during this time. The Persians were in control for many years. Several stories in the Old Testament are said to come from this time. Eventually the Greek ruler Alexander the Great defeated the Persians. That started a long period of Greek influence called the Hellenistic period. It was during this time that Egyptian and Syrian rulers also fought over and took turns controlling the homeland of the Jews. For a time, the Jewish people rebelled and they regained control of their own land and rededicated the temple in 165 B.C.E. Eventually, the Romans conquered the land, and were the ruling power when Jesus was born.

The story of the Jewish revolt mentioned above is told in books known as 1 and 2 Maccabees. These books don't appear in all versions of the Bible. (Yes. there *are* different versions of the Bible that contain different lists of books.) Most Protestant Bibles have the same sixty-six books, thirty-nine in the Old Testament and twenty-seven in the New Testament. Other Bibles, especially those read by Roman Catholic and Orthodox Christians, have additional books known as the Apocrypha, or Deuterocanonical Books. A detailed summary of these different lists can be found on pages 28-29 of *Lutheran Study Bible*.

How is it possible to have more than one Bible? The same way we have different denominations and Christian traditions. Traditions have a lot to do with this. The Hebrew Scriptures have the same books as the Protestant Old Testament. Martin Luther, the great church reformer, included the Apocryphal books in a separate section of his Bible translation. He said that these books were good to read and study, but they did not have the same authority as the books that were included in the Jewish canon or list. The Greek version of the Jewish Scriptures (called the Septuagint) contains many of the other books (the Apocrypha). Roman Catholic Bibles followed the Greek version, for the most part. So, those Bibles contain more books than the usual Protestant Bibles.

Over 500 years separated the end of the exile and the birth of Jesus

Quiet time
Not ruling them
Serves
not a lot of faith

Jewish revolt and rededication of the temple in 165 B.C.E.

- What do you imagine life might have been like for Jewish people living in Judah and Jerusalem during the many years leading up to the birth of Jesus?

Different versions of the Bible have different lists of books

- What more would you like to know about the different lists of books found in different versions of the Bible?

Review the timeline on pages 30-32. Notice especially the "Powers and Kingdoms" that dominated the homeland of the Jewish people from around 500 B.C.E. to the time Jesus was born.

Review the chart called "Different Canons of the Hebrew Bible (Old Testament)" on pages 28-29. How are the main sections of the Jewish Tanakh (Hebrew Scriptures) different from the sections we generally use in Christian Bibles? What differences do you see in the lists of books belonging to different Christian Bible versions?

Look at the list "Thirty Key Old Testament Stories" on page 2094. How many of these do you recognize from the first nine chapters of *The Greatest Story?* Check out some of the Key Verses listed. Consider adding them to your "Mark It" reading for this chapter.

PICTURING THE STORY

As you watch the story unfold in the video, reflect on these questions:

- What are the three ideas or themes you especially want to remember about the Old Testament part of the story?
- How has your understanding of the meaning of the Old Testament changed, if at all?
- If someone asked you why Christians read the Old Testament, what would you say?
- What part of the story is most interesting to you so far? Why? Which part would you like to know more about?

SINGING AND PRAYING THE STORY

The book of Psalms found in the Bible was the worship book of the people of Israel. The psalms are prayers and songs used to offer praise and thanks to God, ask for God's help, seek God's forgiveness, remember God's actions, and even complain or cry out to God. Christians use the psalms the very same way as we worship and as we reflect on our relationship with God.

Psalm 22

Jesus prayed the first part of this prayer for help as he hung on the cross.

Here is an example of how the New Testament looks back to the Old Testament. Compare Psalm 22:1 to Matthew 27:46 or Mark 15:34. How does the tone of the psalm change from beginning to end?

Psalm 103

This psalm of praise focuses on God's acts of deliverance.

How is God described in this psalm? How does the message of this psalm connect with themes introduced in this chapter? Which words strike you the most? Why?

MARK IT

Choose one or more of the following passages from today's section of the story to read during the coming week. Mark your reading using the marking method shown here.

Isaiah 61:8-11   Deuteronomy 30:11-20

Micah 4:1-7   Zechariah 9:9-10

Marking Your Bible

Make notes about the questions and insights you have as you read your Bible. The following symbols might be helpful.

* A chapter or verse important to me

! A new idea

√ A passage to memorize

? Something not clear to me

∞ God's love

℗ A promise from God

≈ Something that connects with my experience

† My relationship with God

↔ My relationships with others

Next Time

In chapter 10 we will turn to the New Testament portion of *The Greatest Story.* In the Gospels we will meet Jesus, the one who is at the center of the story.

To help you prepare for the next chapter, you are encouraged to read the following pieces from *Lutheran Study Bible.*

- New Testament Overview, pages 1597-98
- The Gospels and Acts Introduction, pages 1599-1600
- Matthew Introduction, pages 1604-1606
- Mark Introduction, pages 1659-1660
- Luke Introduction, pages 1694-1695
- John Introduction, pages 1752-1753

10

THE WORD BECAME FLESH
The Gospels, Part 1

The main character in the greatest story hits the stage

- Explain the phrase "the Word became flesh" in your own words. Is it easier to imagine Jesus as human or as God? Why?

Jesus is God's Word in the flesh

THE WORD BECAME FLESH

(John 1:1-14; Matthew 1:1-17)

The word *gospel* means "good news." The New Testament in the Bible contains four Gospels: Matthew, Mark, Luke, and John. The very first line of the Gospel of Mark, probably the first Gospel to be written, starts with these words: "The beginning of the good news of Jesus Christ, the Son of God" (Mark 1:1). The Gospels tell the good news (gospel) of Jesus. Who is Jesus? The Gospels make the amazing announcement echoed by other writings in the New Testament: Jesus, son of Mary and Joseph, is God's Son and the Messiah (or Christ).

The writer of the Gospel of John says this in a unique way. Just like the beginning of the Old Testament story in Genesis, John looks back all the way to the beginning of time. At the very beginning when God created everything by the Word, the Word (Jesus) was right there with God. And not only that, the Word WAS God. Everything "came into being through him." All life came from, and continues to come from, the Word.

The Word was and is God—this is quite a claim. But then John makes an equally mind-boggling statement: "And the Word became flesh and lived among us, and we have seen his glory" (John 1:14). This Word in the flesh is Jesus. Like no one before or since, Jesus connected heaven and earth. As Christians we proclaim this to be true. Jesus was and is God. And Jesus was also a human being in every sense of the word. He wasn't a spiritual being who only looked like a human being. He was a human being. And he was God come to us in the flesh.

Some of the writings of the New Testament, and probably millions of pages written since, try to explain how this can be. But mainly the Gospels tell the story of Jesus of Nazareth—who he was, what he did, and what he said— and trust the story to capture the readers. The writer of Matthew's Gospel begins by helping us see that Jesus was connected to the family that God called to be a holy people. Look at the family tree described in Matthew 1:1-17. You'll recognize quite a few names from the story you've heard so far. Jesus' family tree includes Abraham and David, but also the prostitute Rahab and the foreigner Ruth. Jesus was born to a Jewish father (Joseph) and mother (Mary). The story of God's people included the promise of a Messiah. Christians believe Jesus is that Promised One.

Jesus was Jewish, born into the family lines of Abraham and David

- In what ways can families be channels of hope and promise? What is most surprising to you about Jesus' family?

JESUS IS BORN (Luke 1–2; Matthew 1)

Some would say that the greatest story begins with Jesus' birth in the manger in Bethlehem. But we've already seen that many important chapters in the story lead up to this wondrous event. And when we get to the Gospels, some are surprised to see that in Mark and John the story of the good news of Jesus does not begin with his birth. (Mark's Gospel begins with Jesus already grown. The same is true in John, once we get past the introduction.) Others are surprised to find that Matthew and Luke don't tell the story of Jesus' birth in identical ways.

In the Gospel of Matthew, the story seems to focus on Jesus' father Joseph. The story tells us that Joseph wanted to dismiss Mary quietly when he discovered she was pregnant (and the child was not his). He didn't want to go through with the wedding. But an angel appeared to him and told him not to be afraid to take Mary as his wife, because the son she was carrying was from the Holy Spirit. Joseph was further instructed to call the boy Jesus, "for he will save his people from their sins." According to the words of the prophet Isaiah, Jesus would also be known as *Emmanuel*, which means "God is with us" (Matthew 1:20-23). Joseph trusted God and took Mary as his wife. By naming the boy Jesus, Joseph adopted the child as his own.

Joseph: Your son will be known as Emmanuel, which means "God is with us"

- When he discovered Mary was already pregnant, Joseph was no longer obligated to marry her. It took courage and trust to go through with the marriage. Where did he get that courage and trust?

Mary: You will be mother of Jesus, the son of the Most High

- What do you think of Mary's response to the news that she would be the mother of God's Son?

In Luke's Gospel, the story of the birth seems to focus on Jesus' mother Mary. An angel appeared and told Mary that God had chosen her to be the mother of a son, whom she was to name Jesus. He would be called "son of the Most High" and would be given the throne of his ancestor David. All those promises of a Messiah in the Scriptures of her people would come true in her son. When Mary wondered aloud how this could happen, she was told that "nothing will be impossible with God" (Luke 1:37). What did she do? Like Abraham and Sarah and Moses and many others before her, she trusted God's promise. She said, "Here am I, the servant of the Lord; let it be with me according to your word."

Jesus was born in a cattle stall in Bethlehem

- Martin Luther called the Bible the manger that holds the Christ child. What do you think he meant by that?

Luke reports that the Roman government, which ruled the area at that time, ordered everyone to be registered in their hometowns. This registration was done so that the people could be taxed. Joseph was a descendant of David, so Mary and Joseph traveled from their home in Nazareth in the north to Joseph's family territory in the south. They went to Bethlehem, which was known as the city of David, to be registered. They couldn't find a room at any local inn, so they ended up bedding down in a cattle stall. Jesus was born there and laid in a feedbox, or manger, filled with straw. Angels announced the birth to local shepherds, who came to see the baby Jesus.

Wise men from the east bring gifts to Jesus

Even though they are often pictured at the birth of Jesus, the wise men actually showed up later. Only Matthew's Gospel mentions these wise men, or astrologers, who came from lands east of Judea, where Jesus was born. Their arrival and meeting with the local King Herod triggered a terrible series of events. Herod reacted badly to the news of a newborn child who might be a rival messiah king. In a fit of jealousy, he ordered the killing of all the boys in Bethlehem who were two years old or younger. But before the massacre, God's angel warned Joseph to get Mary and Jesus out of town. They escaped to Egypt and hid out there, until they heard that Herod had died and it was safe to go home to Nazareth.

JESUS IS BAPTIZED BY JOHN

(Luke 3; Matthew 3)

Very little is known about Jesus' life between his earliest years until he was nearly thirty years old. The Gospel of Luke reports a family trip to Jerusalem to celebrate the Passover festival when Jesus was twelve (Luke 2:41-52). At the end of the festival, probably thinking he was with the neighbors, the family left for home without him. When they discovered he was missing, they rushed back to Jerusalem, where they found him in the temple teaching the teachers. Mary and Joseph had good reason to be worried and angry. But they were also amazed to see their young son doing such a thing. They must have wondered if this was a glimpse of bigger things to come.

When we next see Jesus in the Gospels, he is already grown up. Along with many other Jewish neighbors, Jesus went to the Jordan River to be baptized by his cousin John, who was known as John the Baptist. John had been preaching to crowds and encouraging them to get baptized, along with confessing their sins and repenting (turning away from sin and back toward obeying God). John also told the crowds that someone else more powerful than himself was going to come and baptize people with the Holy Spirit and fire. The powerful one John was talking about was Jesus. Only people didn't know Jesus and his power yet.

Surprisingly, Jesus himself came to be baptized. Now you might be wondering why Jesus, who was God, would need to be baptized. Well, John was wondering the same thing. But Jesus told him his baptism was part of God's plan for him to fulfill all righteousness (Matthew 3:15). What that means is not immediately clear, but as the story unfolds we will find that God's righteousness has to do with God's forgiving love and justice. Jesus could only fulfill God's plan to forgive by identifying fully with sinners—including us!

Jesus was baptized by his cousin John in the Jordan River

- John the Baptist prepared the way for Jesus. Who has prepared the way to Jesus for you?

In his baptism, Jesus identified with sinners

- Complete this sentence: Because Jesus was baptized, I . . .

The Word of God's promise became flesh and lived among us. As the gospel story will reveal, this means that Jesus identified fully with sinners, even to the point of assuming our sin. But that's not all that happened at the Jordan River when Jesus was baptized. The Holy Spirit came down on Jesus, and a voice from heaven said, "This is my Son, the Beloved" (Matthew 4:17). When we are baptized, God's promise is for us too. God's Spirit comes to us, and we become children of God.

JESUS FACES TEMPTATION

(Matthew 4:1-11; Luke 4:1-13; Mark 1:12-13)

In his baptism, Jesus identified with sinners. It's not surprising, then, that right after his baptism Jesus went into the wilderness to meet Satan, the Master of Sin, face-to-face. For forty days, Satan tempted Jesus in the wilderness. You might remember that in Old Testament times, the Hebrew people wandered for 40 years in the wilderness after they left Egypt. They certainly were tested by their ordeal. Most of them never made it to the promised land.

But Jesus was in tune with God, no matter what Satan threw at him. Satan told Jesus to use his power to turn rocks into bread, but Jesus didn't do it. He trusted that God would provide. Satan told Jesus to worship him, and then he could rule the world. To that temptation, Jesus recited the First Commandment: "Worship the Lord your God, and serve him only." Satan told Jesus to "wow" the world by surviving a fall from the very top of the temple. No deal, Jesus said. That's a test I don't need to take. So, Satan got tired of the game and left—for the time being.

Satan wasn't gone for good, of course. He would come back. And he's still around playing his little testing games. Sometimes the evil that Satan stirs up can be a huge mess. We may wonder why God doesn't just crush Satan and stamp out evil once and for all. The Bible wrestles with this question, too. It seems that God allows us to choose good or evil, and with this freedom comes the risk of temptation. However, the Bible makes this clear: God in Christ has defeated evil. Jesus loved us so much that he allowed himself to be tested, so he would be able to help us when we are tested (Hebrews 2:18). His ultimate test came when he suffered and died on the cross. In Jesus' death and resurrection, God crushed the power of Satan forever.

Jesus resisted Satan's temptations in the wilderness

- If you could ask Jesus anything about temptation or facing evil, what would you ask?

Jesus was tested, so he can help us when we are tested

- What do you think about the idea that God allows us the freedom to choose good or evil? What would life be like if we couldn't choose?

JESUS CALLS THE FIRST DISCIPLES

(Luke 5:1-11, 27-32; Mark 3:13-19)

Luke tells us that at the beginning of his ministry, in a synagogue in his hometown of Nazareth, Jesus read from a scroll containing the words of the prophet Isaiah:

The Spirit of the Lord is upon me,
　　because he has anointed me
　　　　to bring good news to the poor.
He has sent me to proclaim release to the captives
　　and recovery of sight to the blind,
　　　　to let the oppressed go free,
to proclaim the year of the Lord's favor.

When Jesus announced that this Scripture was being fulfilled in him, the people in his hometown congregation were excited at first, but then became angry. In fact, they tried to throw him over a cliff and kill him (Luke 4:16-30). Why would these words rile people up so much? Isn't this what God wanted—to bring justice to those who were poor, healing to those who were in pain, and freedom to those who were oppressed?

Jesus' whole life and ministry were about bringing this vision of God into reality. He invited others to follow him and join in this vision, including a close group of twelve. (These twelve followers may symbolize the twelve tribes of Israel.) So, he invited fishermen like Simon Peter, James, and John to leave their nets and follow him. He invited a tax collector named Levi. The twelve he invited included a man named Judas Iscariot, who ended up betraying Jesus. Just like the people God called in the Old Testament, Jesus' followers were real folks, men and women, who showed uncommon faith and courage, common faults, and even a lack of faith at times.

The twelve disciples traveled with Jesus every day. They saw and heard and experienced remarkable things. And many of them went on to do remarkable things in Jesus' name and by the power of the Holy Spirit. Jesus chose them, and Jesus sent the Holy Spirit to choose and to give gifts to disciples in every time and place. "Come, follow me," Jesus says. "Be the voice and the hands, the face and the feet, of the good news."

Jesus proclaimed his mission in the words of the prophet Isaiah

- How would you describe what Jesus' mission was and is?

Jesus chose disciples to share his vision and his work

- What role do Jesus' disciples play in that mission?

Jesus says, "Come, follow me!"

- How do you hear Jesus' invitation to "Come, follow me"?

JESUS HEALS (Mark 5:1-43)

Life has limits. Illness and injury and emotional pain remind us that being human means living with certain limitations. When we are healthy and living in healthy relationships, life can be very good. When we are sick or experiencing physical, emotional, or mental distress, life can be challenging. At those times, we hope for, we look for, and we may even pray for healing.

Jesus used the power of God to bring healing to many

- What kinds of limits have you faced in your life? Do you need healing?

Healing people in distress was a key part of Jesus' ministry. The Gospels are filled with stories of Jesus touching people who were sick, possessed by demons, or dealing with physical challenges. He even touched some who faced the final limitation of death and brought them back to life. The fifth chapter of Mark's Gospel tells of three such healing encounters.

First, Jesus met a man who had an unclean spirit and was living in a grave-yard because he couldn't live near his neighbors anymore. The man was called "Legion," because so many unclean spirits were in him. Jesus ordered the unclean spirits to come out of the man and into a herd of pigs nearby. Then the pigs ran down a steep bank into the sea and were drowned. The neighbors were amazed when they saw the man in his right mind. But the story of the drowned pigs also frightened them so much that they begged Jesus to leave the neighborhood.

Jesus overcame unclean spirits, illness, and even death

- Imagine being present when Jesus heals someone. What emotions would you feel? What questions would run through your mind?

- Jesus had power over illness and death. Christians believe he still does. How is this true?

So, Jesus left for another town, where a local synagogue leader told Jesus that his young daughter was sick and close to death. He asked Jesus to come and lay his hands on her and make her well. Jesus agreed to see the girl, but as he was traveling through town, a woman grabbed his robe. She was hoping that just touching Jesus would heal a hemorrhaging illness she had been suffering with for twelve years. She was right. Her faithful touching tapped Jesus' healing power. Jesus told her, "Daughter, your faith has made you well; go in peace, and be healed of your disease" (Mark 5:34).

When Jesus arrived at the home of the synagogue leader, the young girl was already dead and people were wailing and crying, mourning her death. When Jesus told them that the girl was just sleeping and not dead, their crying turned into sarcastic laughter. It didn't matter. Jesus took the girl by the hand and told her to get up—and she did. The people were overcome with amazement.

JESUS FEEDS THE 5,000

(Mark 6:30-44; John 6:1-51)

Healings were not the only kind of miracles Jesus performed. Keep in mind that Jesus was not only human but God in the flesh. And with God, anything is possible.

Jesus fed 5,000 people with five small loaves of bread and two fish

One day, Jesus and his disciples tried to get away from the crowds that had been gathering everywhere he went. They took a boat to a place they thought would be private, but the crowds spotted them and ran ahead. They were waiting when Jesus and his followers got out of the boat.

The disciples wanted to just send the people away, but Jesus had compassion for them. They had been so focused on hearing Jesus teach or on getting healed, they hadn't even thought about bringing food along with them. So, Jesus told the disciples to give the people something to eat. The disciples must have looked at Jesus and thought the long day had finally gotten to him. It would be expensive to feed such a huge crowd of people, and where would they find food to buy in the first place?

- What does the miracle of the loaves and fish say to you about Jesus? What does it say to you about food in our world?

Jesus told the disciples that they didn't need to spend any money. Instead he took what was on hand—five small loaves of bread and two fish. He blessed the food and broke it. The disciples started passing out the food to the crowd, and it never ran out! After everyone had eaten, the leftover bread and fish filled twelve baskets.

This story is expanded in the Gospel of John. In private Jesus reminded his disciples of the bread that God gave to their ancestors, the Hebrew people, while they wandered in the wilderness. Then Jesus said, "I am the living bread that came down from heaven. Whoever eats of this bread will live forever; and the bread that I will give for the life of the world is my flesh" (John 6:51). This is the same promise we hear at the table of the Lord in Holy Communion: "This is my body, given for you." The Word who became flesh is present in the bread that he himself calls his body. This body of Christ brings us together as one body, Christ's church on earth.

Jesus is the living bread from heaven

- What do you think is a greater miracle—that Jesus could multiply the loaves and fish, or that Jesus gives us his body in the bread of the Lord's Supper?
- What question do you have for Jesus today?

PICTURING THE STORY

As you watch the story unfold in the video, reflect on these questions:

- What do you find most interesting or puzzling about Jesus' birth?
- What question would you like to ask Jesus about his baptism or temptation?
- If Jesus were to appear to you and say, "Come, follow me," what do you think you would do? What would you say?
- How do Jesus' disciples—no matter when and where they live—carry out the mission and ministry of Jesus?
- What does it mean for you to be a disciple?

SINGING AND PRAYING THE STORY

The book of Psalms found in the Bible was the worship book of the people of Israel. The psalms are prayers and songs used to offer praise and thanks to God, ask for God's help, seek God's forgiveness, remember God's actions, and even complain or cry out to God. Christians use the psalms the very same way as we worship and as we reflect on our relationship with God.

Psalm 91

A liturgical psalm that reflects on the image of God as a refuge.

The words of this beautiful psalm portray God as protector. Note the connection between verses 11-12 and Satan's efforts to tempt Jesus into jumping from the top of the temple. How do the promises in Psalm 91 connect to what you know of Jesus' mission and ministry?

Psalm 113

This psalm praises God as one who cares for people who are poor and needy.

How does the message of this psalm connect with the words Jesus spoke in his home synagogue about his mission?

MARK IT

Choose one or more of the following passages from today's section of the story to read during the coming week. Mark your reading using the marking method shown here.

Matthew 6:25-34   Luke 6:27-36
Mark 2:1-12   John 4:1-42

Marking Your Bible

Make notes about the questions and insights you have as you read your Bible. The following symbols might be helpful.

*   A chapter or verse important to me

!   A new idea

√   A passage to memorize

?   Something not clear to me

∞   God's love

Ⓟ   A promise from God

≈   Something that connects with my experience

†   My relationship with God

↔   My relationships with others

Next Time

In chapter 11 we will continue the story of Jesus told in the Gospels.

To help you prepare for the next chapter, you may wish to review or read the following pieces from *Lutheran Study Bible*.

- New Testament Overview, pages 1597-1598
- The Gospels and Acts Introduction, pages 1599-1600
- Matthew Introduction, pages 1604-1606
- Mark Introduction, pages 1659-1660
- Luke Introduction, pages 1694-1695
- John Introduction, pages 1752-1753

11

WHO DO YOU SAY I AM?
The Gospels, Part 2

History kneels at the foot of the cross and rejoices at the empty tomb

Jesus calmed the windstorm on Lake Galilee

- Imagine what it might be like to witness one of Jesus' miracles over the forces of nature. Would this experience make you more or less certain that God exists?

Jesus showed God's power over nature

- What do you think the miracles over the forces of nature say about Jesus?

JESUS STILLS THE STORM (Luke 8:22-25)

One key part of Jesus' ministry was his power to heal people, as we saw in the previous chapter. Jesus also showed power over nature. One day a windstorm hit while the disciples and Jesus were traveling by boat across a big lake, probably Lake Galilee. As the waves pounded the boat and began to fill it with water, the disciples screamed in terror. Fearing they were about to drown, they frantically awakened Jesus. Immediately, he yelled at the wind, and ordered the windstorm to stop. As you might expect, the disciples were amazed. "Who is this," they wondered, "who even has power over the wind?"

Ancient Scriptures said that only God has power over the forces of nature. God tamed the waters of chaos at the time of creation. God sent the flood and then stopped it again. God opened the sea for the Israelites to escape from the Egyptian army. God sent food and water to save them in the wilderness. The disciples in the boat may have wondered if Jesus could have the power of God.

Calming the storm on Lake Galilee was not the only time Jesus showed power over the natural world. Among other things, he turned water into wine at a wedding in Cana (John 2:1-11), walked on the water (Matthew 14:22-33), and ordered a huge catch of fish for the disciples (Luke 5:1-11). The miracles showing Jesus' control over nature weren't reported as often as his miracles of healing. And yet, both types of miracles caused people to be amazed and demonstrated the power of God.

JESUS TEACHES

(Matthew 5:1-12; 22:34-40; Luke 15:11-32)

Besides performing miracles of all kinds, Jesus was also a wise teacher. In fact, the Gospels are filled with Jesus' teachings. One major collection of Jesus' teachings, known as the Sermon on the Mount (Matthew 5–7), includes something we call the Beatitudes. You can read all of the Beatitudes in Matthew 5:1-12, starting with "Blessed are the poor in spirit." Jesus went on in the Sermon on the Mount to teach about the ways of righteousness and the kingdom of God, touching on matters such as anger, worry, forgiveness, prayer, and judging others.

Jesus was a master teacher

One day, a group of teachers of the law known as the Pharisees asked Jesus to name the greatest commandment. He didn't name just one. He answered that the greatest commandments are these: Love God, and love your neighbor as yourself. On these two commandments, he said, hang all the law and the prophets (see Matthew 22:34-40, Mark 12:28-34, Luke 10:25-28).

One of Jesus' favorite ways to teach was to tell stories. We call these stories *parables*. A parable is a short, simple story that teaches a lesson. Through his parables, Jesus taught about life in God's kingdom and what it looks like. Often the stories were told for a particular reason and to address a certain situation. Many times the point of a story was surprising or sharp, prodding listeners to view life and God's promises in new ways.

Jesus often taught by telling stories called parables

• Why are stories such a powerful way to teach?

A good example of such a parable is the story of two brothers and a father, most often called the Parable of the Prodigal Son. You can find this parable in Luke 15:11-32. At first glance, the story seems pretty simple. The youngest son begs his father to give him his share of the inheritance. The father gives it to him. The son goes away and wastes all the money, mostly on partying. (That's the prodigal part—the son was reckless and wasteful.) When he ends up with no money and is forced to eat the slop fed to pigs, the son realizes what a good deal he left behind. So he returns home. He's embarrassed but desperate, and expects to receive the worst from his father. But instead, the father is waiting for him, forgives him, and welcomes him back. He even throws a big "welcome home" celebration. "My son was lost," the father says. "But now he is found."

Parables have a point, and they point us to life in God's kingdom

- What would you say is the point of the Parable of the Prodigal Son?

- Name a powerful thing that you have learned. What teacher or teachers have influenced you the most? Why?

This is a beautiful example of a parent's love. But, wait, there's more to this story. What about the other son? The one who stuck around the whole time to help out on the family farm? Well, he's upset that his father so easily forgives his irresponsible little brother. Can you blame him?

Now if we look back to the beginning of Luke 15, we see that Jesus was surrounded by tax collectors and sinners. Nearby some religious teachers, the scribes and Pharisees, were grumbling, saying, "This fellow welcomes sinners and eats with them" (Luke 15:1-2). Knowing this, who do you think the parable was meant to prod?

The seemingly simple Parable of the Prodigal Son raises profound questions. How are we sometimes like the younger brother, living recklessly or expecting the door to be slammed in our faces if we return home? How are we sometimes like the older brother or the grumbling religious leaders, wanting to control who is in and who is out of God's kingdom or family? This is how Jesus' teachings worked on those who heard him teach in the flesh, and this is how his teachings continue to work on us.

Jesus raised his friend Lazarus from the dead

- How do you hear Jesus' words about the resurrection?

Jesus is the resurrection and the life

- Why do you think some fear Jesus' power over life and death?

JESUS RAISES LAZARUS (John 11:1-44)

Jesus was friends with two women named Mary and Martha, and their brother Lazarus. One day, Jesus got the news that Lazarus was dying. By the time he got to his friends' house, Lazarus was already dead. His body had been wrapped in burial cloths and placed in a tomb. Martha, grief stricken, met Jesus on the road and told him she knew that if he'd been there, he could have saved Lazarus. Jesus then told her that Lazarus would rise again. "I know that he will rise again in the resurrection on the last day," Martha replied. To this Jesus said, "I am the resurrection and the life. Those who believe in me, even though they die, will live, and everyone who lives and believes in me will never die" (John 11:24-26).

When Mary came to see Jesus, she was crying. And that caused Jesus to cry, too. Then he ordered the people nearby to take away the stone that blocked the opening to the cave-like tomb. He yelled for Lazarus to get up and come out of the tomb—and Lazarus did! People took the burial cloths off of Lazarus. But while many of the people who witnessed this miracle were amazed, some of the religious leaders began to plot to get Jesus killed.

JESUS ENTERS JERUSALEM

(Mark 8:27—9:1; Luke 19:28-40)

Eventually, Jesus' journey led him to Jerusalem and his death. He had predicted this day would come. In Mark's Gospel, his prediction comes right after talking with his disciples about what people are saying about him. They said people thought that Jesus was "John the Baptist, Elijah, or one of the prophets." When Jesus asked, "But who do you say I am?," Peter answered, "You are the Messiah."

Jesus predicted he would suffer and die on the cross

Then Jesus told the disciples what was going to happen. He would have to go and suffer and be rejected by the religious leaders. He would be killed, but he would rise again after three days. Peter, the one who had just answered Jesus correctly, started telling Jesus not to talk about his death that way. But Jesus told him to be quiet; he even compared Peter to Satan. God's plan included Jesus facing death on a cross. That cross was something all of Jesus' followers would have to carry. He told the disciples and the crowd: "If any want to become my followers, let them deny themselves and take up their cross and follow me" (Mark 8:34).

- How do you answer Jesus' question: Who do you say I am?
- What do you think it means to carry Jesus' cross?

The last week of Jesus' earthly life began with a ride on a donkey into Jerusalem. Ancient kings of Israel had ridden in procession on noble donkeys, and now Jesus rode through the gates into the city. Crowds lined the streets waving palm branches and crying out, "Blessed is the king who comes in the name of the Lord!" The people had watched Jesus perform miracles and teach for nearly three years. His reputation had grown, and here he was right in front of them, bigger than life. Could he really be the Messiah king who had come to lead them, and maybe free them from Roman oppression?

The people of Jerusalem cheered Jesus as a Messiah king

But not everyone was cheering. Many of Israel's religious leaders were nervous. They weren't convinced that Jesus was the Messiah, and they feared what the Romans rulers might do if the people tried to make Jesus the head of a rebellion against Rome. The Romans allowed the Jewish people and their leaders to worship at the temple in Jerusalem. But if a rebellion started, all bets might be off. The Romans could shut down the temple and make life very hard for the people.

The Jewish leaders feared Jesus might start a rebellion

Jesus shared a final Passover meal with his disciples

- What do Jesus' words, "This is my body and blood," mean to you?

Jesus prayed in the garden of Gethsemane, where he was arrested

- What do you think of Jesus' prayer in the garden of Gethsemane?
- How do you face difficult times?

A LONG NIGHT (Luke 22:1-65)

Many Jewish people were in Jerusalem for the Festival of Unleavened Bread, also known as the Passover. This festival celebrated God setting their ancestors free from slavery in Egypt. Because Jesus was still in the city, and the people were still buzzing about him, the chief priests decided to try to find a way to get rid of Jesus, once and for all. One of Jesus' disciples, Judas Iscariot, took money from the chief priests and the temple police, promising to hand Jesus over to them. On the night of Passover, Jesus met with his disciples in the upper room of a house to celebrate the meal. At this last supper with the disciples, Jesus gave them bread and wine, telling them that these were his body and blood. We celebrate this meal and receive the promise of forgiveness of sins whenever we share in Holy Communion.

Jesus also told the disciples that someone would betray him. He also predicted that, before the night was over, the disciple Peter would deny that he even knew Jesus. Of course, Peter said that this would never happen. But Jesus was right. Before the long night was over, all the disciples had fled, and Peter had denied he knew Jesus—not just once, but three times.

After dinner, Jesus and the disciples (except for Judas) went out to the garden called Gethsemane. Jesus prayed to God while the disciples slept. "Father," Jesus prayed, "if you are willing, remove this cup from me; yet, not my will but yours be done." When he was done praying, Judas showed up with the temple police and pointed out Jesus by giving him a kiss. The police and chief priests arrested Jesus and led him away to face a council that was made up of elders, chief priests, and scribes. Jesus was blindfolded, mocked, and beaten.

Jesus is tried before a council of his own people

A DARK DAY (Luke 22:66—23:56)

Early on the morning after Jesus was arrested, he was brought to a hearing before the assembly of elders, chief priests, and scribes. The Roman government allowed this group to be a kind of ruling council for dealing with internal matters of the Jewish people. The council asked Jesus two key questions. The first one was this: "Are you the Messiah?" Jesus replied, "If I tell you, you will not believe." Then the council asked a second question: "And are you the Son of God?" To this Jesus replied, "You say that I am." Even though he didn't say "yes" to either question, his responses were taken that way, and that was enough for the council to take the next step in the plot to get rid of Jesus.

The council knew that many of the people supported Jesus, so they needed support for their plot. They took Jesus to Pontius Pilate, the Roman governor of Judea, hoping he would see Jesus as a threat. They told Pilate: "We found this man perverting our nation, forbidding us to pay taxes to the emperor, and saying that he himself is the Messiah, a king" (Luke 23:2). Pilate asked Jesus point-blank if he was the king of the Jews. Jesus simply said, "You can say so." Pilate could see no reason to accuse Jesus of anything, but he probably didn't want to upset the people, either. So, he sent Jesus to Herod, the governor of Galilee (the area Jesus came from), who happened to be in Jerusalem at the time. But Herod only made fun of Jesus and didn't find him guilty.

The council brings Jesus to Pilate, the Roman governor

- Politics, religion, God's purposes—all had a role in the death of Jesus. How would you describe the main reason or reasons that Jesus was crucified?

Herod sent Jesus back to Pilate. After lots of arguing and accusations back and forth, the chief priests and leaders of the people begged Pilate to crucify Jesus. They even asked Pilate to release a known criminal named Barabbas, and crucify Jesus in his place. Pilate finally gave up. He washed his hands of the matter, but sentenced Jesus to death by crucifixion. (Crucifixion was used by the Roman government of that time to execute criminals. Those who were crucified were nailed to a cross and left to die from exposure, blood loss, or suffocation.)

Pilate and Herod find no fault in Jesus

Roman soldiers led Jesus on a walk of shame out to a hill called Golgotha, or "The Skull." Along the way, they forced a man named Simon of Cyrene to carry the cross they would use to crucify Jesus. When they arrived at the place, Jesus was put on the cross. Two thieves were crucified at the same time, one on each side of Jesus. To mock him, a sign was placed above his head that named Jesus "King of the Jews." People yelled at him and sarcastically told him to save himself. About three o'clock in the afternoon, Jesus prayed, "Father, into your hands I commend my spirit." Then he died.

Under pressure from the council, Pilate sentences Jesus to death on a cross

- What question would you like to ask someone in this part of the story?

Joseph of Arimathea, one the members of the ruling council, didn't agree with the majority who wanted to see Jesus dead. He asked for the body of Jesus, so he could provide a proper burial. There were tombs nearby, cut out of rock, which belonged to Joseph of Arimathea's family. He placed Jesus' body in one of these tombs. Some women who followed Jesus wrapped his body with burial cloths and put spices and ointments on him. They had to do this quickly, because the Sabbath or holy day was about to begin at sundown. Once the Sabbath started on Friday evening, they were not allowed by Jewish law to do more work to prepare the body.

Jesus dies and is buried in the family tomb of one of the council members

- The cross may be the most common symbol of the Christian faith. What does the cross mean to you?

Jesus rises from the dead!

- Imagine what it must have been like to find Jesus' tomb empty. What might go through your head? What goes through your head and heart today when you think about the resurrection?

Jesus appears to the disciples in various times and places

- How do you recognize Jesus?

"You will be my witnesses"

- How are the chapters of the story of Jesus still being written?

Jesus blesses the disciples and goes up to heaven

RESURRECTION! (Luke 24; John 20–21; Matthew 28:16-20)

When Jesus died and was buried, it probably looked like the end of the story. But the most exciting chapters were yet to come. The Jewish Sabbath ended at sunset on Saturday evening. Early the next (Sunday) morning, the women who had prepared Jesus' body for burial went back to the tomb with more spices. When they got there, they found the stone that had blocked the tomb entrance rolled away, and Jesus' body gone. Two men dressed in dazzling white told the women that Jesus had risen from the dead (Luke 24:4-7).

The women ran and told the disciples the wonderful news. Some didn't believe it. Peter and another disciple ran to the tomb to see for themselves (John 20:1-9). They, too, found only folded up grave cloths in an empty tomb. They went home amazed and probably in a state of shock. They must have wondered if it was really possible that Jesus had risen from the dead, just like he had promised he would.

The disciples weren't left to wonder for very long. In the next hours and days, Jesus appeared to them in various ways and in various places. He walked with some disciples on the road to Emmaus, a small town outside of Jerusalem. At first they did not recognize Jesus, but when they sat down for a meal together, Jesus broke bread and blessed it. When he did that, they could see clearly. It was Jesus! Later, he showed up when the disciples, except for Thomas, were gathered together in Jerusalem. Jesus showed them the marks of the crucifixion on his hands and feet. But Thomas refused to believe Jesus was alive until he could see Jesus face-to-face. Jesus appeared to him, and Thomas believed. Jesus said to him, "Have you believed because you have seen me? Blessed are those who have not seen and yet have come to believe" (John 20:29).

And how would others believe? Jesus told the disciples that they would be his witnesses. He commissioned them to go and "make disciples of all nations, baptizing them . . . and teaching them" all that Jesus had proclaimed (Matthew 28:19-20). He promised to be with them to the end of the age and sent them out to proclaim the message of repentance and forgiveness in his name to all nations. He also promised that God would give them power from on high to do this (Luke 24:46-49).

Finally, Jesus led the disciples out of Jerusalem, as far as Bethany. There he blessed them and then was carried up into heaven. (Christians celebrate this event as the Ascension of Jesus.) The disciples rejoiced and went back to the temple in Jerusalem to give thanks to God (Luke 24:50-53). The story wasn't over, after all. They were going to live out the next chapters.

Background Files (Lutheran Study Bible)

Look at the maps called "The Roman Empire," "Palestine in Jesus' Time," and "City of Jerusalem in Jesus' Time" (2108-2110). Notice how great an area Rome controlled at the time of Jesus. Note where Judea is. Then find Nazareth in Galilee, where Jesus grew up, on the map of Palestine. Also locate Bethlehem, Jerusalem, and Bethany. Use the map of Jerusalem to trace the events of Jesus' last week in the city.

Review the various views of the temple provided on pages 1696, 1697, and 1741. At the time of Jesus, the Roman authorities allowed the Jewish people to continue to worship God in their temple in Jerusalem and celebrate their religious festivals. How did Jesus and his message seem to threaten this arrangement? In 70 C.E. (A.D.), the Romans put down a Jewish rebellion. During that battle, the Romans destroyed the temple, which was never again rebuilt. The Gospels were most likely written after the destruction of the temple in 70 C.E.

PICTURING THE STORY

As you watch the story unfold in the video, reflect on these questions:

- What do you find most remarkable about Jesus' life and ministry? What do you find most puzzling?
- How do you mainly think of Jesus—as miracle worker, healer, wise teacher, Messiah, savior, or other?
- Do you think it was easier for those who saw and knew Jesus in the flesh to believe he was the Messiah, the Son of God? Why or why not?

- What would you like to ask Jesus?
- Why do you think writers decided to tell the story of Jesus in the Gospels? (You might want to see what the writer of John says about this in John 20:30-31.)
- How can you be a "witness" to the gospel (good news) of Jesus?

SINGING AND PRAYING THE STORY

The book of Psalms found in the Bible was the worship book of the people of Israel. The psalms are prayers and songs used to offer praise and thanks to God, ask for God's help, seek God's forgiveness, remember God's actions, and even complain or cry out to God. Christians use the psalms the very same way as we worship and as we reflect on our relationship with God.

Psalm 25

A psalm that gives thanks to God for God's teachings and mercy.

The words of this psalm echo many themes present in Jesus' life and ministry. Imagine Jesus praying this prayer to God. Does that change the way you see or hear the words? What words ring true for you, especially as you think about what God has done in Jesus?

Psalm 72
A royal psalm praising the ideal king.
How does the message of this psalm connect with Jesus, the Messiah king? What words or phrases speak to you?

MARK IT

Choose one or more of the following passages from today's section of the story to read during the coming week. Mark your reading using the marking method shown here.

Matthew 19:16-26   Luke 20:20-26
Mark 12:28-34   John 14:1-31

Marking Your Bible

Make notes about the questions and insights you have as you read your Bible. The following symbols might be helpful.

*   A chapter or verse important to me

!   A new idea

√   A passage to memorize

?   Something not clear to me

∞   God's love

Ⓟ   A promise from God

≈   Something that connects with my experience

†   My relationship with God

↔   My relationships with others

Next Time

In chapter 12 we will see in the book of Acts how the first followers of Jesus continued to tell the good news story about him. They lived out his command to be his witnesses in all the world.

To help you prepare for the next chapter, you may wish to read the following pieces from *Lutheran Study Bible*.

- New Testament Overview, pages 1597-1598
- The Gospels and Acts Introduction, pages 1599-1600
- Acts Introduction, pages 1794-1795

12

YOU WILL BE MY WITNESSES

Acts

Spirit-led followers make sure the Word is heard

YOU WILL BE MY WITNESSES! (Acts 1)

The story of Acts begins where the Gospels leave off. In fact, Acts is actually the second part of a great continuing story started in the Gospel of Luke. You can see the connection in the opening verses of Luke and Acts. The writer created a two-part account of what Jesus taught and everything that happened to him and his followers. He wrote the account for a person named Theophilus (Luke 1:1-4).

Jesus rose to be with God, but not before he gave the disciples some instructions. You might call them marching orders. He told the disciples that they would be his witnesses in "Jerusalem in all Judea and Samaria, and to the ends of the earth" (Acts 1:8). Jesus also made them an important promise: "You will receive power when the Holy Spirit comes upon you." Jesus did not expect the disciples to tell the story on their own or without his help. Jesus would send the Holy Spirit to give them courage and wisdom and the words they would need.

Before the sending of the Holy Spirit, the disciples gathered in a house in Jerusalem. They had an important matter to work out. Since the disciple named Judas had betrayed Jesus and then committed suicide, they needed a replacement for him. They prayed and also cast lots. This was like drawing straws, except that they trusted God to guide this process to the right outcome. In the end, Matthias became the newest of the twelve disciples.

Acts continues the story begun in the Gospel of Luke

Jesus promises to give the Holy Spirit

- Why would you say the promise of the Holy Spirit was so important to the disciples?

they trusted him

Matthias is chosen to join the twelve disciples

- How would you have felt to be chosen as the new disciple?

Honored

The Holy Spirit came to the disciples on Pentecost

- How did Peter make it clear that the story of Jesus was part of the story that God had begun long before?

Peter told the good news story of Jesus, and 3,000 new followers were baptized

- Imagine that you are someone in the crowd on the day the Holy Spirit came upon the disciples. Describe what you hear and see.

People praising God & listening to stories

SOULS ON FIRE (Acts 2:1—5:16)

Fifty days after Passover, according to the Jewish calendar, the disciples were gathered together to celebrate the festival of Pentecost, which was also called the Festival of Weeks. Less than fifty days had passed since Jesus rose from the dead. As they gathered, a sound like wind blew into the room and tongues of fire rested on them. By the power of the Holy Spirit, the disciples began to speak in various languages. People from many different regions, who had gathered in Jerusalem for the festival, heard the disciples speaking in their own languages. Many were amazed, while others thought the disciples must be drunk.

The disciple Peter stood up and spoke for the group. First, he explained that the disciples were not drunk, but experiencing what God had said through the prophet Joel in their sacred Scriptures. God would pour out the Spirit on all people. They would have visions, and everyone who called on the name of the Lord would be saved (Acts 2:16-21). Peter proclaimed that even now God was making good on that promise and pouring out the Holy Spirit on those gathered there. He went on to speak of their ancestor, King David, and compared him to Jesus. "God has made him [Jesus] both Lord and Messiah, this Jesus whom you crucified" (Acts 2:36), Peter said.

Then Peter called on the crowd to repent and to be baptized in the name of Jesus Christ so that their sins could be forgiven. About 3,000 people who heard Peter's message were baptized right then and there. The number of Jesus' followers grew quickly. The believers shared all they had, and they spent time together in the temple worshiping and at home giving thanks and praise to God. And just as Jesus had power to heal people, the disciples received the power in the Spirit to heal people, too. One day, Peter healed a man who was crippled and had lain outside the temple begging every day. Acts reports that all the apostles did wonders like this among the people (Acts 5:12-16).

But mainly, Peter and the others continued to tell the story of Jesus. Peter spoke right near the temple where people gathered. He told them that Jesus fulfilled the promises God made to their ancestors Abraham and Moses. God chose Jesus and glorified him, but many had chosen not to believe Jesus was the Messiah and killed him, the Author of life. Peter's preaching didn't sit well with the local rulers, elders, and chief priests. Peter and John were hauled into a trial before the same council that had plotted to get rid of Jesus. The council warned Peter and John not to keep spreading the story about Jesus. But Peter and John said, "We cannot keep from speaking about what we have seen and heard" (Acts 4:20).

The council leaders let them go, and Peter and John just went back and gathered with other believers and prayed once again for the courage and strength to keep telling the story no matter what. Their prayers were answered. The Holy Spirit came upon them again and made them speak even more boldly.

The council could not keep Peter and John from telling the story

- Why was being a witness to the story of Jesus no easy task? What makes being a witness to this story challenging today?

Many choose not to believe Jesus was the Messiah

DEATH THREATS (Acts 5:17—9:2)

It wasn't going to be easy. Being Jesus' chosen witnesses was a daily struggle. At one point, a high priest had the apostles arrested and thrown in prison. But they miraculously escaped and started preaching again. They were brought before the council, which debated whether to put them to death or not. One council member, a Pharisee named Gamaliel, talked the others out of this. He was afraid the deaths of the disciples might cause a riot. So, the council had them whipped and released instead. The disciples were actually honored that they could suffer and put their lives on the line for Jesus.

The disciples kept telling the story of Jesus, even when threatened with prison or death

- How do you think you might react if you were threatened with imprisonment or even death for speaking up for Jesus? What's the bravest thing you have ever done?

One of Jesus' followers was a man named Stephen. He was "full of grace and power" and "did great wonders and signs among the people" (Acts 6:8). But some argued with Stephen and were jealous of him. They made up some lies to tell the council. They said Stephen was speaking against the temple, and proclaiming that Jesus was going to destroy the place and change the customs Moses had handed down from God.

A follower named Stephen was stoned to death

- Have you ever felt persecuted? Have you ever persecuted or made fun of someone else because of what he or she believed?

When asked if the accusations were true, Stephen gave a passionate speech to the council. He recalled the history of the Jewish people, from God's call of Abraham to God calling Moses to lead the people out of Egypt. He reminded the council that their ancestors had also turned away from God, making idols to worship and rejecting the prophets who tried to proclaim God's word to them. Stephen's words made members of the council so angry that they took him outside the city and started to throw stones at him. Even as he was dying, Stephen called out to God: "Lord, do not hold this sin against them" (Acts 7:60).

A Pharisee named Saul
persecuted and arrested
many followers

One of the leaders who approved of the stoning of Stephen was a Pharisee named Saul. He led a persecution against his Jewish neighbors who claimed to be followers of Jesus. He went house to house and dragged Jesus' followers, both men and women, off to prison. And he didn't stop there. He even asked the high priest for permission to go all the way to Damascus, far to the north, to round up any followers there.

Jesus calls Saul to stop persecuting the church

- What a turnaround Saul had on the road to Damascus. Do you know of anyone whose life has been turned around? How did this turnaround happen?

A NEW VISION (Acts 9:3—11:18)

One day, Saul, the persecutor of the followers of Jesus, was headed north to do his dirty work at the synagogue in Damascus. But as he traveled, he was knocked down by a flash of light and heard a voice ringing in his ears: "Saul, Saul, why do you persecute me?" Naturally, Saul wanted to know who was talking. The reply came, "I am Jesus, whom you are persecuting." Saul was also told by the voice to go to Damascus, where he would be told what to do next. Because the light had blinded him, Saul had to be led into the city.

After three days, a follower named Ananias was told in a vision to find Saul and lay his hands on him, so he could see again. Ananias had heard of Saul's reputation, so he didn't want to go and help him. But the Lord assured Ananias that Saul was going to have a whole new vision. Ananias obeyed. When he laid his hands on Saul, Saul could see again. Immediately he started telling his story and the story of Jesus in the city's synagogues. His reputation as a preacher of the gospel spread, and soon he was targeted by the very same persecutors he had previously led. He escaped Damascus and went to Jerusalem, but the disciples there were afraid of him.

The gospel is for both Jews and Gentiles

- Why would anyone want to put limits on the gospel? Do you think the gospel is meant for everyone? Why or why not?

Despite persecution and danger, the church was beginning to get a foothold in Judea and Samaria. And Saul was not the only one having visions. The disciple Peter was told in a vision to go to visit a Roman army officer named Cornelius. This centurion, commander of one hundred soldiers, was known as a man who respected God and gave money to the poor. While on his way to see Cornelius, Peter had a strange dream. In the dream, God said it was acceptable to eat things that Peter had been taught were unclean, according to the law of Moses. When Peter arrived, Cornelius and his people were already gathered and waiting to hear what Peter had to say. While Peter was still speaking, the Holy Spirit surprisingly (even to Peter) was poured out on the people and they were baptized. These events led Peter to realize that the message about Jesus and the promises of God were not meant only for his Jewish brothers and sisters. God's good news was also meant for Gentiles (non-Jews), such as Cornelius and his family.

When he returned to Jerusalem Peter reported his vision and his telling of the good news to the Gentiles. At first many questioned him, but then they realized that "God has given even to the Gentiles the repentance that leads to life" (Acts 11:18). This was really a new vision for the early church. For a time the debate about whether the gospel was for both Jews and Gentiles kept going. A council in Jerusalem discussed and addressed the matter (see Acts 15). Saul, who was also known as Paul, was convinced that Jesus had called him to bring the good news to the Gentiles.

Saul brings the good news to the Gentiles

- What kind of vision do you think might be needed in the church today? How would you know such a vision was coming from God?

GOSPEL ROADS (Acts 13–20)

The first generation of Jesus' followers lived in exciting and challenging times. Yet in spite of danger and opposition they kept telling the story. They witnessed to Jews and Gentiles as they preached in Jewish synagogues and outside the temples of Greek and Roman gods. At the new and growing church in Antioch, Paul and his friend Barnabas were prayed for and sent off on what became the greatest gospel road show of all time. They traveled by boat and by foot all across Asia Minor and the cities of Greece and back again. Paul made at least three journeys like this, and his teaching and preaching helped create many new communities of faith.

Paul takes the gospel on the road

But the work was not easy. Often Paul's preaching stirred up crowds. Sometimes he was opposed by Jewish religious leaders, and sometimes he was arrested and imprisoned by Gentile officials in the cities he visited. In one place, after Paul healed a crippled man, the crowd claimed Barnabas was the Greek god Zeus and Paul was the god Hermes come in human form (Acts 14:8-12). Even while he was witnessing to the crowd about the true God, opponents came and dragged him out of town, stoned him, and left him for dead. All in a day's work for Paul!

Eventually, Paul and Barnabas went separate ways, and Paul was joined instead by Timothy and Silas. They took the gospel to Asia Minor, to places like Derbe and Lystra, Phrygia and Galatia. In the northern Greek city of

Paul and other apostles faced intense opposition

- Imagine traveling with Paul as part of his gospel road show. What would have been most exciting? Most scary?

Philippi, they met a woman named Lydia at a worship service outside town by the river. She was captivated by Paul's preaching, became a follower of Jesus, and welcomed Paul and Silas to her home. At Philippi, Paul and Silas were also arrested and thrown in jail. But during the night, an earthquake rattled open the prison doors. The jailer was about to kill himself, thinking his prisoners had escaped. Paul assured him that everyone was accounted for, and told him the story of Jesus. The jailer and his whole family believed and became followers of Jesus.

Paul's preaching and teaching started many churches

- How do you think the message of the gospel can reach people today? What has changed since the time of Paul? What, if anything, is still the same?

- What do you think of Paul's statement that God is the one in whom we live and move and have our being?

Paul also traveled to the beautiful Greek city of Athens, with all of its impressive temples to the gods. Paul preached a powerful sermon right in front of the Areopagus, a place where the people of Athens met to discuss matters of religion and morals. He pointed to the monument built to an unknown god, and told them about the God he knew. He told them about the living God who has come down to save. And quoting from a Greek poet, he said that in this God "we live and move and have our being" (Acts 17:28).

The gospel road show continued in places like Corinth and Ephesus, where Paul started a riot when he preached outside the temple of Artemis. Even so, a church began in the city. That was true in almost all of the places Paul visited. He left behind groups of followers who formed churches. He wrote letters to these newly founded churches, and many of these letters became part of the New Testament.

GOSPEL ON TRIAL (Acts 21–26)

After three long trips preaching and teaching about Jesus in Greece and Asia Minor, Paul returned to Jerusalem carrying an offering collected from churches during his travels. This offering was intended to support people who were poor and suffering in Jerusalem. Paul was warned it would be dangerous to go there, but danger never stopped him. After meeting with James and other leaders of the church in Jerusalem, Paul went to the temple to worship with his Gentile traveling companions. But some who were opposed to Paul and his teachings started a riot and got Paul arrested. He was dragged out of the temple and almost killed on the spot.

Paul was given a chance to speak to the crowd, so he told his story. "I am a Jew, born in Tarsus of Cilicia," he began. He told how he was educated according to the ancestral Jewish law and became a persecutor of the Way, meaning the followers of Jesus. But he also witnessed to the change that took place in his life and how he became a believer in Jesus, who had called him to bring the good news to the Gentiles. Paul was taken to the army barracks near the temple, to be whipped and interrogated. But when the officer in charge realized Paul was a Roman citizen, the beating stopped.

Paul faced a hearing before the council of Jewish leaders, who got in a big argument over Paul and his message. Fearing the council members were going to tear Paul to pieces, the Roman soldiers guarding him took him back to the barracks. When the officer in charge got wind of a plot to ambush Paul, he sent Paul to Caesarea, escorted by armed guards, to appear before the Roman governor Felix.

Paul told his story to Felix, who didn't find him guilty of any crime. But he kept Paul under house arrest for two years, as a favor to Paul's Jewish opponents. But when Festus replaced Felix as governor, Jewish leaders renewed their accusations against Paul, and once again he had to plead his case. Festus offered to send Paul back to Jerusalem to stand trial. Knowing that to do this meant almost certain death, Paul instead made an appeal, which was his right as a Roman citizen, to have his case heard before the Roman emperor. Festus also sent Paul for a hearing before King Agrippa, and there Paul boldly tried to talk Agrippa into becoming a follower of Jesus. But finally, Agrippa told Festus to send Paul to Rome to get his hearing before the emperor.

Paul returns to Jerusalem and is arrested at the temple

- Paul had many identities—he was an expert in Jewish law, a Roman citizen, a follower of Jesus, missionary to the Gentiles. Which one of these do you think he thought was most important? Why?

A Roman officer sends Paul to the Roman governor in Caesarea

- How do you identify yourself? Which part of that identity is most important? Why?

As a Roman citizen, Paul appeals to the emperor to avoid trial in Jerusalem

Paul survives a storm at sea on his way to Rome

- How would you describe the journey you are on? How is it like or unlike Paul's journey?

Paul lives in Rome for two years, teaching and preaching the gospel

- The church today traces its roots back to the church described in the story of Acts. What do you think has changed? What is still the same?

LAST STOP ROME (Acts 27–28)

Now Paul's gospel road show set sail for Rome. He was put on board a ship with more than 200 other prisoners. Along the way a terrible windstorm struck the ship, nearly sinking the ship and killing everyone. Paul helped to keep up everyone's spirits on board as the ship drifted for over two weeks, until it ran aground on the Island of Malta. There Paul miraculously survived the bite of a poisonous snake and cured a local man named Publius when he prayed for and laid his hands on him.

After three months on Malta, Paul finally made it to Rome. While there, he was kept under house arrest, but was allowed to meet with people, including the leaders of the Jewish community in Rome. Once again he told his story. These leaders had not heard all the negative things that the leaders back in Jerusalem were saying about Paul, and they wanted to hear what he had to say about Jesus. Some heard and believed, and others didn't. And the same arguments that met Paul's missionary preaching in the past continued to appear.

According to Acts, Paul stayed on in Rome for more than two years, proclaiming the kingdom of God and teaching about the Lord Jesus Christ. The Bible doesn't say what happened to Paul after that. Many assume that he was executed in Rome under the Emperor Nero, but some believe he may have been released, going on to preach in Spain or even returning to the churches he started in Asia Minor.

Background Files (Lutheran Study Bible)

Look at the maps "Paul's Missionary Journeys" and "The Early Church and Key Locations in Acts," pages 2111-2112. Trace Paul's journeys, noting some of the key locations mentioned in Acts. What must it have been like to travel the region?

Review the map that lists the cities and countries named in Acts 2 (page 1797). Jews from all these regions were in Jerusalem to celebrate Pentecost.

Look at the chart "Key People in Acts" on page 1825. Read about these people, using the Bible text references listed on the chart.

PICTURING THE STORY

As you watch the story unfold in the video, reflect on these questions:

- What must it have been like to experience the outpouring of the Holy Spirit on the Day of Pentecost?
- When have you experienced, or when do you experience, the presence of God's Spirit?
- What do you find most surprising or amazing about the beginning of the church?
- What question would you like to ask Paul or one of the other early leaders of the church?
- Why or how does the church of Jesus Christ survive today? How can it grow?
- Is the road you are "traveling" a gospel road? If not, what kind of road are you on?

SINGING AND PRAYING THE STORY

The book of Psalms found in the Bible was the worship book of the people of Israel. The psalms are prayers and songs used to offer praise and thanks to God, ask for God's help, seek God's forgiveness, remember God's actions, and even complain or cry out to God. Christians use the psalms the very same way as we worship and as we reflect on our relationship with God.

Psalm 138

A psalm that gives thanks to God for protection and strength.
As a Jew and an expert in Jewish law, Paul would have known the psalms. Imagine Paul praying this psalm in the evening after a long day on the road telling the story of Jesus. What part do you think prayer played in Paul's life? Why?

Psalm 96

This psalm of praise is also known as an enthronement psalm that praises God as ruler.
The greatest story is the story of a God who saves. What might the followers of Jesus say is the "new song" (verse 1) that they sing to the Lord?

MARK IT

Choose one or more of the following passages from today's section of the story to read during the coming week. Mark your reading using the marking method shown here.

Acts 4:1-22   Acts 17:16-34
Acts 8:26-40   Acts 21:37—22:29

Marking Your Bible

Make notes about the questions and insights you have as you read your Bible. The following symbols might be helpful.

* *   A chapter or verse important to me
* !   A new idea
* √   A passage to memorize
* ?   Something not clear to me
* ∞   God's love
* ℗   A promise from God
* ≈   Something that connects with my experience
* †   My relationship with God
* ↔   My relationships with others

Next Time

In chapter 13 we will explore the letters Paul wrote to a number of early Christian churches and individuals. All the letters of Paul were written at least a generation or two before the four Gospels and Acts, so they give us several pictures of how the story of Jesus was being told and interpreted very early on in the church. You might not be surprised to find out that these were times of bold witness and faithfulness to the gospel as well as controversies and disagreements.

To help you prepare for the next chapter, you may wish to read the following pieces from *Lutheran Study Bible*.

* The Letters of Paul Introduction, pages 1849-1850
* Romans Introduction, pages 1851-1852
* 1 Corinthians Introduction, pages 1874-1875
* 2 Corinthians Introduction, pages 1896-1897
* Galatians Introduction, pages 1911-1912
* Ephesians Introduction, pages 1920-1921

* Philippians Introduction, pages 1929-1930
* Colossians Introduction, pages 1936-1937
* 1 Thessalonians Introduction, pages 1942-1943
* 2 Thessalonians Introduction, pages 1948-1949
* Philemon Introduction, pages 1969-1970

THE POWER OF GOD FOR SALVATION

The Letters of Paul

The man, the mission, and the message

Paul's letters teach the gospel in a powerful way

- What kinds of things do you learn from reading letters or personal e-mails?

God's salvation is for Jews and Gentiles alike

- Why do you think Paul's message angered some and gave great hope to others? How does his message strike you?

A NEW MAN WITH A NEW MESSAGE

(Galatians 1:11—2:21; Philippians 3:2-11)

We heard about Paul's gospel road show in the previous chapter when we looked at the greatest story as it is told in the book of Acts. Now we turn to hearing the story through the letters of Paul that made their way into the New Testament. We can learn a lot by reading these letters. They give us glimpses into the life of Paul and some of the people and churches he met as he preached and taught the gospel story of Jesus. We get a sense of the deep and life-changing impact the good news story of Jesus had on those who heard and responded to Paul's preaching.

Paul knew that who he was and where he came from were important parts of his story. He never forgot that although he had persecuted the early Christians, Jesus had forgiven him and sent him to share the good news. He constantly told about God's grace and the way the good news had power to change human lives. In Paul's letter to the Galatians, he reminded them of his Jewish background and his ongoing debate with other leaders in the early church who were also followers of Jesus.

Some Christian believers in Galatia thought new male Gentile believers needed to be circumcised according to Jewish custom. To this, Paul said a firm "No!" Even though he had been trained as a teacher of the law and followed all the Jewish customs, Paul's message from Jesus was clear: God's message of salvation was for both Jews and Gentiles (non-Jews). When God sent Jesus, things changed. The good news of God's mercy was for everyone.

Gentiles did not have to follow all the Jewish customs and traditions in order to be put right with God and become part of God's people. Paul said, "a person is justified not by the works of the law but through faith in Jesus Christ" (Galatians 2:16). This was a radical new message spoken by a changed man.

Gaining Christ meant everything to Paul

- What do you think it means to gain Christ?

Paul reminded his friends in Philippi of his background as well. He had been the most righteous follower of the Jewish faith, upholding the law perfectly. Still, everything he gained in his former life he came to regard as nothing, compared to knowing Jesus. And even though Paul suffered many hardships to keep on telling the gospel story of Jesus, suffering didn't matter to him—and not even death made him afraid—because he had gained Christ and knew he would share in Jesus' resurrection from the dead (Philippians 3:2-11).

Paul is named as author of 13 New Testament letters

- What thoughts or questions do you have about whether Paul actually wrote all the letters that bear his name?

TO ALL GOD'S BELOVED (Paul's letters to churches)

Thirteen of the 27 books of the New Testament name Paul as author. All of these books are actually letters, most of them written by Paul to followers in the places he had preached and taught the gospel. He wrote one of his longest and most influential letters to the church in Rome. Although Paul had not founded or visited this church himself, the letter to the Romans makes it clear that he intended to visit soon. Paul also wrote letters addressed to individuals, such as his friend Philemon and his coworker Timothy.

Most of the letters that name Paul as author were certainly written by him, but there is disagreement about whether he wrote all of them. Why is that? Well, in ancient times, it was acceptable for someone to write a letter in the name of an important teacher to carry on that person's insights and teachings. This means that some of Paul's letters might have been written by one of his closest students. There are other clues to this as well. Paul's letters were written in Greek. Careful comparison of all of the letters in the original Greek shows some differences in writing style and word choice, and some ideas found in certain letters are not found in the letters that are clearly written by Paul.

Although we can't prove these things once and for all, the teachings found in letters that bear Paul's name give witness to the story of Jesus as the Risen Lord. Apart from the teachings of Jesus himself, Paul's teachings are the most influential of all in the New Testament.

Next to Jesus, Paul is the most important teacher in the New Testament

When we look at the letters themselves, what's amazing is that Paul didn't write long books (as far as we know) or major essays. His important teachings are found in these occasional letters, written to real people who had real questions or were experiencing challenging issues. Often he wrote because he had received news, probably by letter, about something happening in the church. Sometimes he wrote to give his opinion about a dispute. For example, in the church at Corinth, some of the followers seemed to be teaching that the Holy Spirit had given some followers better gifts for serving God than others. He told them that all gifts were given to build up the whole body, meaning Christ's church. He said the greatest gift is love (1 Corinthians 13).

Paul's letters encourage, teach, and challenge the followers of Jesus

- Why do you think Paul's personal letters to churches and to individuals became part of the Bible?
- What kind of a letter would you like Paul to send to you or to your church?

I AM NOT ASHAMED OF THE GOSPEL

Most importantly, Paul's letters focused on Jesus and the gospel story. In his letter to the Romans, Paul calls the gospel "the power of God for salvation to everyone who has faith, to the Jew first and also to the Greek" (Romans 1:16). ("Greek" was another name for Gentile.) He told the followers in the church at Galatia that the gospel broke down all barriers. In Christ, he said, "there is no longer Jew or Greek, there is no longer slave or free, there is no longer male and female; for all of you are one in Christ Jesus. And if you belong to Christ, then you are Abraham's offspring, heirs according to the promise" (Galatians 3:28-29).

The gospel is the power of God for salvation

- How does Paul help connect the beginning of the greatest story to Jesus? How does he help you see yourself in the story?

The promise Paul spoke about is the promise of being saved by God's grace through faith. Paul, in fact, ties the whole story together here. For Paul, those who belong to Christ by faith are part of God's people who stretch all the way back to Abraham and Sarah. That goes for every Christian believer today as well. What an amazing promise that is. But Paul goes back even further—all the way back to Adam and Eve in the Garden of Eden. With them sin came into the world, but with Jesus the free gift of God's grace is given for all (Romans 5:12-21).

All who have faith in Christ are part of God's people

Only Jesus can make us acceptable to God

- How does it make you feel to know that Paul struggled with sin each day?
- How would you define the word *grace*?

Does that mean we never struggle with sin anymore? No, Paul says that sin is still part of the story of our lives every day. He admitted that this was true in his life as well. He said, "I do not do the good I want, but the evil I do not want is what I do" (Romans 7:19). Sound familiar? Paul also said "all have sinned and fall short of the glory of God" (Romans 3:23). Adam and Eve sinned by trying to be like God. Well, Paul reminds us that no one can be like God. We can't outrun sin or make ourselves acceptable to God by following the law perfectly or by praying every minute or by doing good works (though praying and doing good works are encouraged). Only Jesus can make us acceptable to God. "There is therefore now no condemnation for those who are in Christ Jesus" (Romans 8:1). That's the powerful good news, the gospel, which Paul was not ashamed to preach and teach.

We are justified by grace and made new in Jesus

- How do you see the connection between God's grace and our freedom?

POWERFUL MESSAGES
(Selected passages from Paul's letters)
The passages below provide a few more examples of the important teachings that fill every one of Paul's letters.

"[We] are now justified by his grace as a gift, through the redemption that is in Christ Jesus" (Romans 3:24). To be *justified* means to be made acceptable to God. Nothing we can do can make us justified. That's why God sent Jesus to redeem us. *Redemption* means that Jesus paid for our sins on the cross. Or to say it another way, God showed us mercy and forgiveness in Jesus, and rescued us from the powers of sin and death.

"We have been buried with him by baptism into death, so that, just as Christ was raised from the dead by the glory of the Father, so we too might walk in newness of life" (Romans 6:4). Baptism connects us to both the death and resurrection of Jesus. Jesus died to take away the sins of the world. Being baptized connects us to this promise. Our sins are drowned in baptism. That's like dying and being buried. But because Jesus died and rose to new life, God promises in baptism that we too will experience new life. God gives us new life now, and promises that we will share a new resurrected life with Jesus when we die.

"For freedom Christ has set us free, . . . only do not use your freedom as an opportunity for self-indulgence, but through love become slaves to one another" (Galatians 5:1, 13). Who doesn't like the sound of freedom? But the freedom Christ gives is not the freedom to act in any old way we want. The freedom Christ gives is the freedom to love our neighbor. In fact, it's the kind of love that puts the needs of our neighbors, family, friends—and even strangers—ahead of our own needs. How can we do that? Well, we can't do it on our own or by our own power or strength. Jesus sent the Holy Spirit to empower us in this new life to love others. When we live by the Spirit, Paul says, our lives will show the fruits of the Spirit, which is evident in things like "love, joy, peace, patience, kindness, generosity, faithfulness, gentleness, and self-control" (Galatians 5:22-23).

"Put on the whole armor of God . . . take the shield of faith, with which you will be able to quench all the flaming arrows of the evil one. Take the helmet of salvation, and the sword of the Spirit, which is the word of God" (Ephesians 6:11, 16-17). We are saved by grace, but life has a way of trying to keep us from truly believing or living according to that promise. Sometimes it feels like evil, or the evil one, is on the attack. That's when we remember that God has given us the Spirit and the word to protect and guide us.

- How does the armor of God fit you? What may need to be strengthened, tempered, tightened, or added?

The best way to experience Paul's teachings is by reading each letter. As you read, take your time. Paul was a very skilled and passionate writer. Keep in mind that he wrote his letters for a specific purpose or to address a certain situation. Imagine yourself in the congregation listening to Paul's letter. Do you feel encouraged by his words? Are you surprised, excited, or challenged? Underline words or phrases that are especially meaningful to you. Write down thoughts or questions that come to mind. Pray for God's Spirit to guide you, just as the Spirit gave courage and wisdom to Paul.

Background Files (Lutheran Study Bible)

Look at the maps "Paul's Missionary Journeys" and "The Early Church and Key Locations in Acts" on pages 2111-2112 in *Lutheran Study Bible*. Then look at a list of Paul's letters. Match the names of some of the letters with the locations on these maps.

Review the Introductions to 1 and 2 Timothy and Titus, pages 1952-1953, 1959-1960, and 1965. These letters are listed along with the letters of Paul. Together they are called the Pastoral Letters or Pastoral Epistles, because they deal with issues around leadership in congregations.

PICTURING THE STORY

As you watch the story unfold in the video, reflect on these questions:

- Imagine what it must have been like for a congregation started by Paul to receive a letter from him.
- Paul wrote his letters to address very specific circumstances. Why do you think the message of his letters is still so important to Christians today?
- What idea or theme stands out to you most in Paul's letters?
- Which of Paul's letters would you like to read and study more closely? How do you plan to do this?
- If you were to write a letter explaining what you believe, what would you say? Who would you want to tell?

SINGING AND PRAYING THE STORY

The book of Psalms found in the Bible was the worship book of the people of Israel. The psalms are prayers and songs used to offer praise and thanks to God, ask for God's help, seek God's forgiveness, remember God's actions, and even complain or cry out to God. Christians use the psalms the very same way as we worship and as we reflect on our relationship with God.

Psalm 121

This is a psalm expressing trust in God.
According to the writer of the psalm, where does help come from? How is this similar to what Paul says about being saved or justified (made acceptable to God)?

Psalm 131

Another trust psalm.
This seems to be the prayer of one who knows his or her place in relation to God. Why would Paul like verse 3? What does that verse say to you?

MARK IT

Choose one or more of the following passages from today's section of the story to read during the coming week. Mark your reading using the marking method shown here.

Romans 8:31-39   Philippians 2:1-11
1 Corinthians 13:1-13   Colossians 3:1-17

Marking Your Bible

Make notes about the questions and insights you have as you read your Bible. The following symbols might be helpful.

* ∗   A chapter or verse important to me
* !   A new idea
* √   A passage to memorize
* ?   Something not clear to me
* ∞   God's love
* ℗   A promise from God
* ≈   Something that connects with my experience
* †   My relationship with God
* ↔   My relationships with others

Next Time

In chapter 14 we will explore more New Testament writings. Some are called letters, while others read more like sermons or collections of teachings.

To help you prepare for the next chapter, you may wish to read the following pieces from *Lutheran Study Bible*.

* General Letters and Revelation Introduction, pages 1972-1973
* Hebrews Introduction, pages 1974-1975
* James Introduction, pages 1992-1993
* 1 Peter Introduction, pages 1999-2000
* 2 Peter Introduction, pages 2007-2008
* 1 John Introduction, pages 2012-2013
* 2 John Introduction, pages 2019-2020
* 3 John Introduction, pages 2021-2022
* Jude Introduction, page 2023

SO GREAT A CLOUD OF WITNESSES
General Letters

Keeping the faith, running the race, living in love

The General Letters linked a new generation of Christians with the past

The letters are named for important apostles

- Imagine living in the second or third generation of Christians after Jesus had lived, died, was raised from the dead, and then ascended to be with God. What kinds of issues or questions do you think you might be dealing with?

Good Storyteller

LINKING PAST AND FUTURE

A group of letters in the New Testament, often called the "General Letters," were most likely written in the generation or two after Jesus' disciples, also known as apostles, had died. The messages in these letters appear to be aimed at a generation of Christians who are moving into a future that is uncertain. They faced persecution from the outside and false teachings that threatened to divide them from the inside. They wanted to know what it means to live as followers of Jesus.

The letter to the Hebrews was at one time thought to be written by Paul, but early church leaders were uncertain about this and most modern scholars doubt the connection. The assumed connection with Paul, however, is probably the reason why Hebrews is placed first among the general letters. The seven letters that remain are named after three of the most outstanding apostles (James, Peter or Cephas, and John) and a lesser-known one (Jude). The order of these letters (James, Peter, and John) may be based on Galatians 2:9, where Paul lists the three in that sequence and speaks of them as "pillars" of the church in Jerusalem. That means Jude comes last.

The names of these letters associate them with early disciples of Jesus and leaders of the church. James is likely named for James, the brother of Jesus (Mark 6:3), who became an apostle (Galatians 1:19) and leader of the church in Jerusalem (Acts 15:13). Peter is named for the apostle Peter, also known as Simon Peter. His name comes first when the twelve disciples are listed in the New Testament (for example, see Matthew 10:2; Acts 1:13). John likely is the disciple John, son of Zebedee (Matthew 4:21). Jude likely refers to one of the brothers of Jesus, who became an apostle (1 Corinthians 9:5). In the letter of Jude, the writer calls himself "brother of James" (Jude, verse 1), likely referring to the James who was also a brother of Jesus.

As we found out in the previous chapter, in ancient times it was not unusual for someone to write letters or other documents in the name of a person of authority. In the General Letters, it is likely that leaders writing for a new generation wanted to express the teachings and perspectives of the great pillars of the early church. This was like saying that the present and future of the church needed to be built on the most solid pillars who were closest to Jesus. The teachings in these letters have stood the test of time and continue to speak to each new generation of Christians.

The church is built on solid pillars who knew Jesus

- In what way is the church always built on and linking the past with the future?

A CLOUD OF WITNESSES
(Hebrews)

Right from the beginning of this letter, which is really more like a sermon, the greatest story takes center stage. "Long ago God spoke to our ancestors in many and various ways by the prophets, but in these last days he has spoken to us by a Son" (Hebrews 1:1-2). A lot is said in that opening. Though written in Greek, the letter's reference to "our ancestors" points to the Hebrew (Jewish) people, the descendants of Abraham and Sarah. And so it appears that this letter was written to second-generation Greek-speaking Christians, many of whom seem to have had a Jewish background.

Hebrews was written to Greek-speaking Christians

Jewish connections seem important to this writer, who often quotes from the Hebrew Scriptures, and compares Jesus to important figures from the Old Testament. Jesus, he says, is "worthy of more glory than Moses," who "was faithful in all God's house as a servant." But Jesus "was faithful over God's house as a son" (Hebrews 3:3-6). Jesus is also compared to the high priest of Israel. One of the most important duties of the high priest was to "offer gifts and sacrifices for sins" (Hebrews 5:1). As high priest, Jesus did not offer animal sacrifices for sins. He offered himself and his own blood to provide forgiveness of sins for all people (Hebrews 9:24-28; 10:12-14).

- Think back to earlier chapters. How do you see Hebrews tying parts of the greatest story together?

Hebrews makes one of the boldest statements of what Lutherans have called "theology of the cross." God is not revealed in sacrifices in the holy sanctuary, but on the cross—the last place anyone would look to find out about God's will, purpose, and heart.

Jesus died on the cross to bring a new covenant

• What's new about the covenant that Jesus brings?

According to the writer of Hebrews, Jesus became "the guarantee of a better covenant" (7:22). The first covenant God gave to Moses and the people of Israel was based on laws and commandments. But Jesus brought the new covenant that the prophet Jeremiah said God would give to the people (Hebrews 8:8-13; Jeremiah 31:31-34). The new covenant, made possible by the death of Jesus, reveals the true depths of God's love for all people. The new covenant will be written in the people's hearts, and God will no longer remember their sins.

Faithful witnesses from the past are cheering us on

The writer of Hebrews looked to the Hebrew Scriptures for examples of great faith. He mentions Abel, Enoch, and Noah (Hebrews 11:4-7), and especially Abraham (11:8-22) and Moses (11:23-28) as great examples of faith. He also names others we heard about in earlier parts of the story—Rahab, Gideon, Samson, Samuel, and David (11:29-40). Like a great cloud of witnesses, these faithful ancestors surround new generations of God's people. The writer pictures these faithful ones like a crowd at a big sporting event, cheering on the new followers, including us, as we run the race of faith. And as we run, we have an advantage because we can keep our eyes on Jesus, "the pioneer and perfecter of our faith" (12:1-2).

• Who makes up the "cloud of witnesses" in your life? Who is cheering you on and encouraging you in your faith walk or run?

Running the race of faith apparently was not easy for those addressed by the letter to the Hebrews. The community was living through various trials, including persecution for being followers of Jesus (10:32-34). It also seems that this generation of Christians expected Jesus to come back at any time, but the delay of that "Day" (10:25) made it all the more important for them to continue to encourage each other and to be disciplined about running the race of faith.

✝ DOERS OF THE WORD (James)

According to tradition, this letter is identified with James, the brother of Jesus and leader of the Jerusalem church until he was put to death just before the Jewish war of 66-70 C.E. (see Galatians 1:19; Acts 15:13-21). But it seems more likely that an unknown author wrote the letter many years after James died, and dedicated it to this hero of the faith. The letter is addressed to "the twelve tribes in the Dispersion." The meaning of the "twelve tribes" is unclear. It may refer to the early Christian community in relation to the people of Israel. The "Dispersion" refers to Jewish people who had moved or been forced to move (dispersed) from their homeland all over the Mediterranean world.

James was written to an early church community facing trials

The author wants to provide wisdom, based on the wisdom that is a creative gift of God. This "wisdom from above is first pure, then peaceable . . . full of mercy and good fruits" (3:17). Such wisdom helps believers fight temptations, recognize false teaching, and be doers of the word. James encourages believers not to be "hearers who forget but doers who act—they will be blessed in their doing" (1:25). To emphasize this point, the writer goes so far as to say that "faith by itself, if it has no works, is dead" (2:17). James points to Abraham as an example that "a person is justified by works and not by faith alone" (2:22-25).

James encourages believers to be doers of the word

- God gives wisdom (Proverbs 2:6), and wisdom leads to right living. How do you see this kind of wisdom in James?
- What do you think it means to be a "doer of the word"? What things can and should be changed in the world?

The story of the early church was a story of enduring in the face of trials. James touches on this right at the beginning (1:2) and throughout the letter. James warns that those who make friends with the world are enemies of God. Instead, believers are to give their lives to God and purify their hearts. That means taking care not to judge one another or speak evil of one another. It also means not putting trust in earthly wealth because it will disappear. The end of the letter focuses on the themes of patience and prayer. As time goes by and Jesus hasn't returned, waiting with patience and enduring suffering becomes more important. One way to face the waiting is to turn to God with prayers of thanksgiving and prayers for healing and forgiveness.

- Why do you think Luther said it was important to keep the focus on Jesus' death and resurrection?

Martin Luther once described the letter of James as "an epistle of straw." Why did he say this? He believed that witness to Jesus Christ and his cross and resurrection were the heart of the great story of the Bible. Because Jesus is only mentioned in two verses (1:1; 2:1) in James, and the letter doesn't talk at all about Jesus' death and resurrection, Luther said James didn't offer enough of what was central to the Christian faith. But James also reminds us that God's wisdom is a gift implanted in believers (1:21). With this gift of wisdom, we have the freedom and the power to use God's gifts to change those things that can and should be changed.

*Because of Jesus,
Christians now are also
God's holy people*

*Holy living is marked
by suffering and right
conduct*

- Is a person's identity based more on who he or she is, or what he or she does? Why?

GOD'S OWN PEOPLE (1, 2 Peter)

Like the letter of James, 1 and 2 Peter were written in the name of a famous apostle. Still, the identity of the writer is uncertain. Many believe that the letters likely were written some years after the apostle Peter had died. These letters are addressed to many churches. The provinces mentioned in 1 Peter 1:1-2 are all in Asia Minor. The letters focus on issues that the growing churches were facing toward the end of the first century. Those issues included living as God's people, dealing with suffering and hardship, combating false teachers, and getting ready for the day when Jesus would return.

For the author of 1 Peter, new life and new identity are key themes. New life comes from God, who has given us a "new birth into a living hope through the resurrection of Jesus Christ from the dead" (1:3). New identity is explained by drawing on images from God's chosen people, Israel. The author says that the Christian believers are to be "a holy priesthood." But they do not offer animal or grain sacrifices as priests. Instead, they offer "spiritual sacrifices acceptable to God through Jesus Christ" (2:5). Like God's people Israel, Christians are a holy people set apart by God to reflect the light of God, rather than the darkness of the world.

What does new life look like for God's holy people? It takes the form of honorable and ethical conduct. It exercises freedom to love and serve and not to do evil (2:11-17). It follows the example of Jesus, who suffered for the sake of others. This kind of servant attitude should guide the way wives and husbands treat one another with respect and consideration. The writer of 1 Peter believed that the "end of all things [was] near" (4:7), which made it all the more important to live according to God's will and not according to all sorts of earthly desires (4:1-5).

The author of 1 Peter also talks about the "fiery ordeal" that the community of faith was facing (4:12). We don't know for certain what was causing suffering in the community, but the writer assured the people that the suffering was not a disgrace, but a way to serve and glorify God.

In the letter of 2 Peter, the writer warns believers not to listen to false prophets and teachers who were trying to lead them away from the truth (2 Peter 2:1-22). Their messages are described as "waterless springs and mists driven by a storm" (2:17).

The writer of 2 Peter also told readers to keep a lookout for the final days that were coming. Some may have been thinking that Jesus was slow about coming back, but the writer says that "with the Lord one day is like a thousand years, and a thousand years are like one day" (3:8). The Lord is patient, not slow, in giving time for "all to come to repentance" (3:9). The day of the Lord will come like a thief, the writer says, and the earth will be melted with fire. But rather than live in fear of the end, believers are encouraged to live holy and godly lives, look forward to the new heaven and new earth to come (3:11-13), and "grow in the grace and knowledge of our Lord and Savior Jesus Christ" (3:18).

Keep watch for false teachers and the Lord's return

- What do you think is meant by false teaching in these letters? Can you think of an example?

- What do you hope it will be like when Jesus returns?

TRUTH AND LOVE (1, 2, 3, John; Jude)

Ancient tradition associates the three letters of John with the apostle John, but no one can say for certain who wrote them. First John is more like an essay or sermon than a letter. It isn't addressed to any person or group in particular. The very first verses of 1 John contain several words that are also found in John 1:1-18—words such as *beginning, see, word, testify, life, revealed, Father, Son*. Because the letters of John and the Gospel of John share key words and phrases like these, as well as several themes and images, many believe that the letters were written by members of a faith community that was deeply connected to the Gospel of John.

The letters of John share many themes with the Gospel of John

The first and perhaps most important theme in 1 John is who Jesus is and what he has done. The writer calls Jesus "the atoning sacrifice for our sins, and not for our sins only but also for the sins of the whole world" (2:2).

- What is the truth about Jesus? What is the truth about us?

Jesus came to offer forgiveness, because all are sinful. "If we say that we have no sin, we deceive ourselves, and the truth is not in us" (1:8). (You may have heard these words during a worship service.)

1 John focuses on the truth about Jesus and showing God's love

The writer of 1 John also argues against the false teachings of some who said Jesus was a spiritual being who only seemed to be human. Jesus came in the flesh, the writer says, so that "every spirit that confesses that Jesus Christ has come in the flesh is from God" (4:2). This is similar to a key theme from the Gospel of John: "The Word became flesh and lived among us" (John 1:14). In 1 John, those who do not teach that Jesus was God come in human flesh are called antichrists (4:3; 2:18-22).

- In your opinion, why was showing God's love so important in the early church? Why is it still important?

Another key theme in 1 John is God's love made real in the love of Jesus' followers. Hate is part of living in darkness, but God's light shines in those who love others (2:3-11). The writer refers to Jesus' commandment to love one another (3:23), the commandment given to his disciples in the Gospel of John (13:34-35). Showing God's love is the way others know we are Jesus' followers.

Watch out for false teachers!

The short letter of 2 John is addressed by "the elder to the elect lady and her children" (1:1). The elder is an unknown church leader, and the "elect lady" may refer to the whole congregation or to an actual woman who hosted the church in her home. Once again, the themes of walking in love and rejecting false teaching are introduced.

Third John also emphasizes this theme of truth over falsehood. The writer (elder) expresses joy in hearing that a person named Gaius is teaching the truth. But the writer warns about false teachers who spread false rumors about the elder's true teaching.

When you think of false teaching, what comes to mind? How can you know what is false and what is true?

This theme of false teaching and how to respond to it continues in the short letter of Jude. The writer has heard that "intruders have stolen in among you . . . who pervert the grace of our God" (verse 4). Apparently some were teaching that it doesn't matter how a person lives, because God is forgiving and gracious. The writer uses all kinds of colorful names for these false teachers, including "wandering stars, for whom the deepest darkness has been reserved forever" (verse 13). Because these "worldly people . . . are causing divisions" (verse 19), the believers are to pray, remain in the love of God, and keep their eyes on Jesus and the promise of eternal life.

PICTURING THE STORY

As you watch the story unfold in the video, reflect on these questions:

- What questions do you have about what life must have been like in the early church?
- What new idea or theme stood out to you most in these letters? Why?
- What idea or theme was challenging or even confusing for you? Why?
- Which of these letters would you like to read and study more closely? How do you plan to do this?
- What do you think was the biggest threat to the early church? What do you think is the biggest threat to the church today?

SINGING AND PRAYING THE STORY

The book of Psalms found in the Bible was the worship book of the people of Israel. The psalms are prayers and songs used to offer praise and thanks to God, ask for God's help, seek God's forgiveness, remember God's actions, and even complain or cry out to God. Christians use the psalms the very same way as we worship and as we reflect on our relationship with God.

Psalm 111
This hymn of praise explains the relationship between God and humans.
Name the different things that this psalm says God has done. How do these actions define God's relationship with us? How is the theme in verse 10 played out in the words of the letter of James?

Psalm 141
A prayer for help.
Imagine a community of Christian believers praying this prayer. What might be threatening them? Who might the "wicked" be, and what are their "wicked deeds" (141:5)? What kinds of "traps" (141:9) might have been laid for this group of Christian believers?

MARK IT

Choose one or more of the following passages from today's section of the story to read during the coming week. Mark your reading using the marking method shown here.

Hebrews 11:1-3   1 John 4:7-21
1 Peter 2:1-10   James 2:14-26

Marking Your Bible

Make notes about the questions and insights you have as you read your Bible. The following symbols might be helpful.

*   A chapter or verse important to me

!   A new idea

√   A passage to memorize

?   Something not clear to me

∞   God's love

Ⓟ   A promise from God

≈   Something that connects with my experience

†   My relationship with God

↔   My relationships with others

Next Time

In chapter 15 we will explore the book of Revelation.

To help you prepare for the next chapter, you may wish to read or review the following pieces from *Lutheran Study Bible*.

- The General Letters and Revelation Introduction, pages 1972-1973
- Revelation Introduction, pages 2026-2027

COME, LORD JESUS!
Revelation

Ending with a new beginning

It's the revelation of Jesus Christ

- What have you heard about the book of Revelation?

Revelation comes from a Greek word that means "to reveal"

IT'S A REVELATION! (Revelation 1)

We've reached the final episode of the greatest story, and what an ending it is! The book of Revelation is like the fireworks at the end of a day of celebration. It's filled with images and visions that boggle the mind. In fact, that's what has made Revelation both fascinating and confusing—not to mention popular. Who doesn't want to know the answer to questions about how the world will end or about how the battle between good and evil will turn out?

It's easy to get caught up in these questions and miss what the central message of Revelation is all about. Look at the very first verse of the book. This is the "revelation of Jesus Christ." All the bold and dramatic visions in Revelation come back to this: the Christian life centers on Jesus Christ. It will be helpful to keep that in mind when some of the scenes in the story seem strange or confusing. In fact, remembering that Christ is in the center is helpful when things turn upside-down for us in real life.

The title "Revelation" comes from the very first word in the book, the Greek word *apokalypsis*. The style of ancient writing that uses visions and images and focuses on end times is called *apocalyptic*. Our word *apocalyse* is often used today to mean an end-of-the-world catastrophe. But *apokalypsis* simply means "revelation," and refers to a revealing or unveiling of something previously hidden.

- John was banished because of his faith. What would that be like?

"I am the first and the last, and the living one"

- What do you think you would do if you met Jesus face-to-face, even in a vision?

The writer of the book, who received this revelation, was named John. He probably was a leader of several Christian communities in Asia Minor (in what is now western Turkey) in the late first century. During this time, Roman authorities demanded that emperors be worshiped as gods. It's likely that John's preaching and teaching of the gospel got him in trouble with these authorities. He was sent off to the Island of Patmos in the Aegean Sea (1:9). That's where he had a revelation and wrote it down. He addressed his letter to "the seven churches that are in Asia" (1:4, 11).

In his vision, John saw one "like the Son of Man" (1:13). This "Son of Man" was the risen Jesus, who told John, "Do not be afraid; I am the first and the last, and the living one. I was dead, and see, I am alive forever and ever" (1:17-18). There are similar words in 1:8: "'I am the Alpha and the Omega,' says the Lord God, who is and who was and who is to come." *Alpha* and *Omega* are the first and last letters of the Greek alphabet. They are used here to claim that God is the one who holds the story together from beginning to end, even the end yet to be written.

John's vision included letters to seven churches

- Which church would you say faced the biggest challenge? Why?

SEVEN (Revelation 2–3)

"Seven" is an important number in the book of Revelation. This isn't surprising, because in the ancient world the number symbolized perfection and held the mystery of creation and the world. Seven lampstands represented the seven churches that John addressed in his vision. John knew about these churches in western Asia, and perhaps even served as a teacher and leader for them. Each church received a message that spoke directly to its circumstances at that time.

The church in Ephesus had been faithful in getting rid of evildoers and false teachers, but had forgotten that love was at the core of what it meant to live as Christians. The church in Smyrna had been rich, but was under attack. It faced persecution and suffering, but John's vision promised the crown of life if the believers could be faithful until death. The church at Pergamum was living "where Satan's throne is" (2:13). This is a good example of the kind of code language used in Revelation. It meant that the people in Pergamum were surrounded by a culture heavily influenced by Rome, which symbolized evil. John warned them about eating food sacrificed to Roman gods (idols) and doing immoral things in the name of religion.

The Christians in Thyatira had been faithful, but they were in danger of falling under the influence of leaders who said it was okay to compromise their values in order to fit in with the society around them. John gave a wake-up call to the church in Sardis. The people there went through the motions when they met for worship, he said, but showed no real Christian commitment in their daily lives. The church in Philadelphia was poor and not very influential. Yet, in spite of being persecuted, they had been enduring. John encouraged them to keep it up.

The churches were challenged to remain faithful

The church in Laodicea was a wealthy, complacent congregation that thought highly of itself because of its success. But making a religious show is not real faith, and John's message to this church was sharp and biting: "Because you are lukewarm, and neither cold nor hot, I am about to spit you out of my mouth" (3:16).

These churches faced real hardships and persecution in the late first or early second century. They also faced the kinds of issues that Christian communities of faith face today—complacency, lack of commitment, and mistaking empty rituals for faithful discipleship. The letters to the churches were part of a vision, but their messages were about real-world stuff.

In your opinion, what are the biggest challenges facing your community of faith or the Christian church in general?

WORTHY IS THE LAMB
(Revelation 4–7)
John's vision next turned toward heaven. There he saw all kinds of creatures and a group of white-robed elders worshiping and praising God night and day. They sang to one who was seated on a throne, which was surrounded by a rainbow that looked like an emerald:

Only the Lamb can open the scroll

> "You are worthy, our Lord and God,
> to receive glory and honor and power,
> for you created all things,
> and by your will they existed and were created" (4:11).

God is the creator. There's that theme again. Although John's vision looked at the end and future of all things, here is an important reminder of the beginning of all things. God is at the beginning of all things, and guess what, God will be at the end of all things, too.

- Why do you think people are so interested in visions of future destruction?

The vision then turned to an image of a lamb (that's Jesus) and a scroll. (Early in the greatest story, the blood of a lamb saved the people from death when they were in Egypt. Jesus is called the Lamb to remind us that his blood saves people from sin.) What did that scroll say? John wanted to know, but when no one could open the scroll and look into it, he was sad enough to weep (5:3-4). That's probably a clue for all of us who think we can understand God's plans fully. Only the Lamb can open the scroll. Jesus stepped forward to do what humans cannot do for themselves. So the Lamb was praised as the one who was "slaughtered" and was now "worthy" to receive wisdom and power and might (5:12).

Six seals are opened and release visions of destruction and hope

- What truth about life was revealed when the first six seals were opened?

Next the Lamb began to open the first six of seven seals on the scroll, and all kinds of things came out. Four different horses appeared—white, red, black, and pale green—with four riders, sometimes called the Four Horsemen of the Apocalypse. This is similar to a vision of the prophet Zechariah (Zechariah 6:1-7). So what were the horsemen bringing? There are lots of symbols to wade through, but the message is all about security. The attacks of the horsemen demonstrated that the people couldn't find security in governments or national defense, in the rule of society, or in wealth. Death would come to everyone. But for those who had died in the faith, those martyrs who remained faithful in the face of persecution, there was still a message of hope. The sixth seal added an exclamation point to all of the others. A huge earthquake came and caused the sky to fall and sent everyone into hiding. But there is no escaping the final statement that comes in the form of a question: "Who is able to stand?" (6:17). The answer: no one.

The faithful are gathered to worship the Lamb

- If you were being persecuted for your faith in Jesus, how might this part of the vision give you hope? Do you see hope in it for your own life today?

Suddenly, a new vision appeared. John saw a perfect number of servants who had been sealed. There were twelve thousand from each of the twelve tribes of Israel—144,000 in all. God's people included the faithful of Israel. To them were added a huge multitude from every nation, tribe, and people. And all were singing, "Salvation belongs to our God . . . and to the Lamb!" (7:10). The gathering of the faithful worshiped God day and night. The Lamb would be their shepherd, and God would wipe away all their tears (7:15-17).

THE COSMIC BATTLE
(Revelation 8–20)

When the Lamb opened the seventh seal on the scroll, seven even more devastating visions were let loose on the earth. Seven trumpets blown by seven angels represented God's judgments. The trumpets blew out fire and hail on the earth, and a mountain splashed into the sea. A star fell into a third of the rivers of the earth, and poisoned anyone who drank from them. Great darkness came when the sun and moon and stars grew dimmer. But that was only the beginning. Out from a bottomless pit came an army of locusts and horses with human faces and tails like scorpions. And a huge army of two million cavalry killed a third of humankind. But even all of this terrible destruction wasn't enough to convince those who survived to repent.

The seventh seal released terrible destruction

In the vision, two witnesses were sent to call people to repent, but a beast from the pit killed the witnesses. The image of the beast in Revelation can stand for anything opposed to the Lamb, but the original readers of Revelation probably associated it with the Roman Empire. The seventh trumpet started a round of singing and praise to God, which was followed by more thunder and an earthquake. This was followed by visions of a woman, her child, and a dragon (perhaps referring to the church, Jesus, and Satan). Other beasts also appeared, causing hardship for all left on earth. One of the beasts marked everyone's forehead with the number 666, a number that symbolizes evil or imperfection. Many suspect that John's use of this number was also a code for the Roman Emperor Nero, who was known for his horrible torture and slaughter of Christians.

The mark of the beast (666) stood for Roman Emperor Nero

- Is the battle between good and evil in Revelation what you expected? Why or why not?

As if things hadn't gotten bad enough, John's vision also included seven angels pouring out bowls of God's wrath, ending with hundred-pound hailstones (16:21). The vision of God's judgment then turned on an evil woman who sat on a scarlet beast that had seven heads and ten horns. (Rome was built on seven hills, so this reference probably would have been clear to the first readers of Revelation.) Revelation 18 contains a funeral hymn for Babylon, another symbol for Rome. Remember Babylon? In the Old Testament, Babylon destroyed Jerusalem and the Jewish temple, and forced many of God's people into exile. This funeral song is followed by songs of rejoicing in heaven (19:1-10).

- What have you heard about the end of the world? What do you believe?

Finally, another white horse appeared on the scene with a rider called
"Faithful and True" (19:11) and given the name "The Word of God"
(19:13). This rider defeated the armies gathered to make war against him.
Then another angel came down and grabbed the dragon (the devil) and
threw him into the bottomless pit for a thousand years. After that happened, many who had given their lives because of their faith were raised to
rule with Christ for a thousand years. After a thousand years passed, Satan
was released, but then defeated and burned in the lake of fire forever. Those
whose names were not recorded in the book of life were also tossed into the
lake of fire. The great cosmic battle between God and those opposed to God
was now over.

MAKING ALL THINGS NEW (Revelation 21–22)

At the conclusion of the great battle, John sees a vision of God's glorious
victory over the powers of evil. A new heaven and a new earth replace the
first earth. A holy city, a new Jerusalem, comes down out of heaven from
God (21:1-2). John's vision is a fulfillment of what was promised in Isaiah
65:17-19. God will live with the people. Death and pain and tears will be
no more. God will make all things new. The new Jerusalem is built with
the most beautiful and precious stones. And the city doesn't need a temple,
because its temple will be the very presence of "the Lord God Almighty and
the Lamb" (21:22).

*God promises to make
all things new*

• What part of John's vision
of a new heaven and a new
earth stands out for you?
Why?

An angel shows John a river of life flowing from God's throne. It sounds like
the healing river that flowed from the temple in the vision of the prophet
Ezekiel (Ezekiel 47:1-12). John now sees the tree of life (a reminder of the
Garden of Eden at the beginning of the greatest story) growing by the river
of life, with twelve kinds of fruit and leaves that are for the healing of the
nations (Revelation 22:1-2). No sun or moon is needed, because God will
be the light forever.

*Jesus is the beginning
and the end of the story*

Finally, John sums up the entire series of visions with God's declaration: "I
am the Alpha and the Omega, the first and the last, the beginning and the
end" (22:13). Jesus is the beginning of the story (see John 1:1-2), and Jesus
is the end. The past, the present, and the future are all centered in him.
That's the message of Revelation for believers of all generations. Whatever
happens, Jesus the Lamb will be there, making all things new and living
among God's people.

Only God knows what will happen for certain, but many have tried to predict the future by interpreting the meaning of John's vision. They have claimed that Revelation was written to warn about events that will happen, even during their lifetimes. But that's not the point of the book, and throughout the centuries these speculations have again and again failed to come true.

Revelation has three key messages. First, God is in control of history, and the Christian life is centered on Jesus. Second, the terrifying visions provide a warning to those who are falling away from faith. And third, the visions of triumph offer encouragement and hope to those who are oppressed, persecuted, or feeling powerless in a hostile world.

The closing words of Revelation include an invitation and a prayer. The invitation is "Come . . . take the water of life as a gift" (22:17). Jesus invites us to come and follow, to receive all of God's gracious gifts. The prayer is "Come, Lord Jesus!" (22:20). We pray for Jesus to come again, proclaiming that we want to be part of God's kingdom now and for all time. These closing words are a fitting ending to the greatest story!

- Why do you think so many people use Revelation to try to interpret current events?

Come, Lord Jesus!

- Do you see Revelation as more of a warning or a promise? Why?

PICTURING THE STORY

As you watch the story unfold in the video, reflect on these questions:

- What would you like to ask John about himself or his vision?
- What makes the book of Revelation most interesting to you? Why do you think it has been so popular?
- What do you see as the most important message of the book?
- What more would you like to learn about Revelation? How will you go about doing that?
- What do you think of Revelation as the ending to the Bible, the greatest story?

SINGING AND PRAYING THE STORY

The book of Psalms found in the Bible was the worship book of the people of Israel. The psalms are prayers and songs used to offer praise and thanks to God, ask for God's help, seek God's forgiveness, remember God's actions, and even complain or cry out to God. Christians use the psalms the very same way as we worship and as we reflect on our relationship with God.

Psalm 149
A hymn of praise to God.

With Revelation in mind, who might sing this song of praise? Who do you think are the "faithful ones" mentioned in this psalm?

Psalm 130
This is the prayer of someone who has sinned and is asking for help.

Notice the theme of waiting in the psalm. Where do you see this theme of waiting in the book of Revelation? How do we wait? What are we waiting for?

MARK IT

Choose one or more of the following passages from today's section of the story to read during the coming week. Mark your reading using the marking method shown here.

Revelation 7:9-17   Isaiah 65:17-25
Revelation 21:1-8; 22:1-7   1 Thessalonians 5:1-11

Marking Your Bible

Make notes about the questions and insights you have as you read your Bible. The following symbols might be helpful.

＊ A chapter or verse important to me

! A new idea

√ A passage to memorize

? Something not clear to me

∞ God's love

Ⓟ A promise from God

≈ Something that connects with my experience

† My relationship with God

↔ My relationships with others

Next Time

In chapter 16 we will review some of the key themes of the New Testament and celebrate our journey through the Bible. We will think about how each one of us is included in the greatest story.

To help you prepare for the next chapter, you may wish to read or review the following pieces from *Lutheran Study Bible*.

- The Small Catechism: A Simple Guide for the Book of Faith, pages 1530-1535
- Lutheran Insights that Open the Bible, pages 1538-1543

16

JESUS PEOPLE
The New Testament Story for Us

Discovering our place in the greatest story

The greatest story continues with us

We are saved by grace through faith

- What do you think about the statement: "The Bible is just a bunch of words on a page if no one reads or teaches or shares it"?

The greatest story is meant for sharing

- What makes it easy, or hard, to believe that you are saved by grace?

BY GRACE THROUGH FAITH IN CHRIST

(Ephesians 2:1-10)

What makes the New Testament "new" is Jesus. But it's not new in the sense of being a replacement for the old, like a new car replaces the old one. The New Testament is a new chapter in the larger story of God and God's people. God's promises to the people in the Old Testament reach fulfillment in the New Testament in Jesus Christ. And while the biblical story comes to a close with the book of Revelation, the greatest story continues as it is told and heard and shared and lived in each new generation. That means we too are part of the greatest story.

The greatest story is a story meant for sharing. In Romans, the apostle Paul asked a question about how we come to hear and know the heart of the story: "Everyone who calls on the name of the Lord shall be saved. But how are they to call on one in whom they have not believed? And how are they to hear without someone to proclaim him? And how are they to proclaim him unless they are sent?" (Romans 10:13-15). Good questions, right? It's God's story, but God sends us out to share it!

The whole story is worth exploring and sharing, but some parts are particularly important. For example, Lutherans talk about the Bible being the book that reveals Jesus Christ to us. The message about Jesus and his cross reveals something profound about God's love for us and also about God's expectations for how we are to love and treat others. And Scriptures teach us that we can only be reunited with God through the death and resurrection of Jesus. That means that we are saved by God's grace as a gift. The letter to the Ephesians summarizes this well: "For by grace you have been saved through faith, and this is not your own doing; it is the gift of God—not the result of works, so that no one may boast. For we are what he has made us, created in Christ Jesus for good works, which God prepared beforehand to be our way of life" (Ephesians 2:8-10).

Notice the order of things. Our good works can't make us right in God's eyes. But we have been made right with God through Jesus. And God empowers us to live faithfully and produces good works in us to care for our neighbor and the world. Keep this in mind as we look at some other important messages in the New Testament.

GO! (Matthew 28:16-20; Romans 12:4-8)

Jesus was a powerful teacher and a great storyteller. But he knew that God's story would need to be taught and retold by his followers when he went away. That's why Jesus, like other teachers of his time, chose a group of students or disciples to be his closest followers. They traveled with Jesus. They watched and learned. But most of all, they were touched and blessed by the experience of being with Jesus, day in and day out. When the time was right, Jesus handed the story over to them.

"Go and make disciples of all nations"

According to Matthew's Gospel, after Jesus was raised from the dead, he instructed his disciples to meet him on a mountain in Galilee, much like when they had listened to his Sermon on the Mount at the beginning of his ministry. When they came to the mountain, they fell down and worshiped Jesus. Jesus spoke to all of them, including some who had doubts about what was happening. He gave marching orders to the disciples: "Go therefore and make disciples of all nations, baptizing them in the name of the Father and of the Son and of the Holy Spirit, and teaching them to obey everything that I have commanded you" (Matthew 28:19-20).

"I am with you always"

- What do you think it means to go and tell? Does this make you nervous, excited, confused, or something else? Why?

- What gifts do you think others might say you have? What part would you like to play in the greatest story?

Along with the command to go, Jesus gave a promise: "Remember, I am with you always, to the end of the age" (28:20). Jesus called his followers to keep telling the story and to keep making new followers by baptizing them. But he didn't expect them to do this work on their own. Jesus would send the Holy Spirit to the disciples to give them courage and many kinds of gifts. Paul talked about those gifts in Romans 12: "We have gifts that differ according to the grace given to us" (12:6). He went on to name some gifts, such as prophecy, ministry, teaching, exhortation (giving sound advice), giving generously, tireless leadership, compassion, and cheerfulness. These are just some of the gifts that God gives.

Go and baptize. Go and teach. Go and tell. Go and use the gifts you have been given. Go with my promise that I will always be with you. Keep the story alive, Jesus says. And he asks: What kind of part will you play in the story?

*The greatest gift of all
is love*

- Have you ever been a "good samaritan" to someone? Has anyone ever been one to you?

*The Samaritan was the
true neighbor*

LOVE! (1 Corinthians 13; Luke 10:25-37; Romans 13:8-10)

In his first letter to the Corinthians, Paul taught about gifts that come from the Holy Spirit. Controversies were brewing in the congregation at Corinth. Some were arguing that their gifts, such as speaking in tongues, were more important than others. They might have gone so far as to argue that they were better Christians because they had these gifts. In response to this situation, Paul said that all of God's gifts are good when used in the proper ways, because they come from the same uniting Spirit. But he said that one gift is the best of all—love!

Loving our neighbor was a common theme in Jesus' teaching. One of the most familiar parables he told was about the love and compassion that one man showed for another. Maybe you have heard of this story, the Parable of the Good Samaritan. (You can read the whole story in Luke 10:25-37.)

On the surface, the story seems pretty simple. One guy stops to help another guy who has been robbed and left for dead in a ditch by the side of the road. But remember, Jesus' parables are stories with a point. The good guy in the story, the one who helped out, was a Samaritan. The Jewish teachers taught that Samaritans were outsiders, and not really God's people.

Jews and Samaritans were not supposed to mix. Guess who Jesus was telling his story to? Right, the Jewish teachers! It probably made them angry that the hero of the story, the one who was a true neighbor, was a Samaritan.

Loving our neighbor is more about *do* than *who.* Our neighbor is anyone in need. But showing love for others is sometimes risky. "Good samaritans" who stop to help, or who get involved with a stranger in need, sometimes end up being injured themselves. Showing love and mercy is hardly ever simple, and sometimes it's not popular, either.

In the letter to the Romans, Paul got right to the point about love: "Owe no one anything, except to love one another; for the one who loves another has fulfilled the law. The commandments . . . are summed up in this word, 'Love your neighbor as yourself'" (Romans 13:8-9). God calls us to love our neighbor. But we don't earn God's grace by loving others—we are freed by God's grace to show love. In other words, the grace of God comes first. Our love flows from the love that God has shown us by sending Jesus to die. This love is both our enabling power and our example. We are part of the most remarkable love story ever.

Love is more about do *than* who

- Why do you think love is more about *do* than *who*?

- How do you understand the connection between the words *love, grace,* and *law*? How might you diagram the connection?

FORGIVE!

(Matthew 18:21-22; Romans 12:9-21)
It's not always easy to love. In fact, sometimes it can be downright difficult. Sometimes someone may hurt us or someone we love so badly, we may say, "I can never forgive that person." Even in those times, God is present in our pain and anger. God knows it is not easy to forgive.

Forgive as often as necessary

- When does not forgiving cost more than forgiving?

Sometimes forgiving costs a lot. But not forgiving can cost even more. That's why Jesus gave a strong answer to the disciple Peter when he asked, "Lord, if someone sins against me, how many times should I forgive? Up to seven times?" Jesus replied, "Not seven times, but seventy-seven times." The number in the Greek may also mean seventy times seven. And in the Bible the number *seven* represents perfection or completeness. So, Jesus was really telling Peter to forgive as often as necessary. There's no limit!

No limit on forgiveness. That's not easy. The apostle Paul didn't let us off the hook, either. In Romans 12 he talks about what genuine Christian love looks like, and he includes forgiveness: "Do not repay anyone evil for evil, but take thought for what is noble in the sight of all. If it is possible, so far as it depends on you, live peaceably with all. Beloved, never avenge yourselves" (12:17-19a). Paul went on to say that Christians should feed their enemies and give them something to drink. "Do not be overcome by evil, but overcome evil with good" (12:21).

Forgiving someone, especially an enemy, may be one of the hardest things to do. But forgiveness is the way of Jesus. Those who follow Jesus take up the cross of forgiveness. It comes with the territory.

SHINE! (Matthew 5:14-16)

Jesus liked to use objects from real life to describe himself and his followers. Twice in John's Gospel, he called himself "the light of the world" (John 8:12; 9:5). It's not surprising that he used a similar image to encourage his followers in Matthew's Gospel. One day as he was teaching, he told his followers: "You are the light of the world. A city built on a hill cannot be hid. No one after lighting a lamp puts it under a bushel basket, but on the lampstand, and it gives light to all in the house. In the same way, let your light shine before others, so that they may see your good works and give glory to your Father in heaven" (Matthew 5:14-16).

Think back almost all the way to the beginning of the greatest story. God's promises to Abraham and Sarah (Genesis 12:1-3) included the promise that their descendants would be blessed to be a blessing to nations. They were to be like a shining light, an example for all other nations. Their descendants, God's people, were to live in a way that would give glory and honor to God. Because of the way they lived and worshiped God, others would be drawn to this God and would come to worship and trust in God as well.

Jesus made the same promise to his followers in Matthew in his Sermon on the Mount. You *are* the light of the world. Not "you could be" or "you might be" the light. You are! It's a promise. So, don't hide the light. Let it shine for all to see. And yes, let them see "your good works," because when they do, they will give glory to God. Trusting in this promise we continue to speak this line, "Let your light shine before others . . . ," during the rite of Baptism to remind the baptized and everyone else that baptism is the beginning of the Christian life. And a life lived according to the baptismal promises is a life that displays good works. We can shine because Jesus shines the light of love and grace in and through us.

"Let your light shine"

- How do you, or will you, shine?

PRAY! (Luke 11:1-10; Philippians 4:6)

The Bible is filled with prayers. God's people pray, and those prayers carry the whole spectrum of human needs and emotions. Jesus himself prayed. In his praying, as in his serving and loving and suffering, he showed us the way. One day one of his disciples asked him point-blank, "Lord, teach us to pray" (Luke 11:1). Jesus answered with a prayer we know as the Lord's Prayer. It was short, only about forty words, but it was packed with meaning.

Jesus taught the disciples how to pray

- What would you like to learn about prayer?

The first words of the Lord's Prayer show that prayer is about relationship. Jesus referred to God as "Father." We are to think of God as a loving parent when we pray. Not everyone has had loving parents, let alone a loving father. That can get in the way of praying to God as Father. But the relationship of parent to child is intended to be the deepest of bonds. Under the best of circumstances, parents provide for, protect, nurture, and love their children. That's what God is all about.

Prayer is about our relationship with God

The Lord's Prayer also "hallows" God, which means it honors God's holiness. In the very first chapters of Genesis, we discovered that God is God, and we aren't. God is holy and mysterious. We can't fully know God's ways, but we trust that God's kingdom will come to us. How? In his *Small*

Catechism, Martin Luther wrote that God's kingdom comes to us "through the Holy Spirit's grace [so that] we believe God's Holy Word and live godly lives here in time and hereafter in eternity" (The Second Petition of the Lord's Prayer).

In the Lord's Prayer, we pray for daily bread, which includes all those things we need in daily life—the essentials, that is. And as we pray for our own needs, we also remember the needs of others. When we pray the Lord's Prayer, we ask for forgiveness, too. Each day we confess that we cannot measure up to God's standards. The more we realize that, the more we realize that we need Jesus and his forgiveness. And, just as praying for daily bread reminds us of the needs of others, praying for God's forgiveness reminds us of those we need to forgive.

Prayer is dialog

• How do we listen to God when we pray?

Finally, in the Lord's Prayer we pray for help to face temptation and trials. We can use all the "armor" of God, but we cannot escape the fact that life can be challenging. All kinds of things conspire to pull us away from God and build walls between us and others. As the apostle Paul reminded his friends in Philippi: "in everything by prayer and supplication with thanksgiving let all your requests be known to God" (Philippians 4:6). Prayer is like the dialog that keeps running throughout the greatest story.

Don't worry about what you will eat, or what you will wear

• What makes you worry? How can you reduce worry? How do Jesus' words help?

HOPE! (Matthew 6:25-34; Romans 8:31-38)

There is so much more to be said about the greatest story, but let's end here with a word about *hope*. It's as good a place as any to complete our journey. One thing that can get in the way of hope is worry about the future. But Jesus said, "Do not worry about your life, what you will eat or what you will drink, or about your body, what you will wear. Is not life more than food, and the body more than clothing?" (Matthew 6:25).

It's interesting that Jesus' words about worry come right after teaching about material possessions. "Don't store up earthly treasures," he said. We can't be devoted both to wealth and to God. Does that mean we can't have faith or live a faithful life if we have wealth? No. But it's hard, Jesus said, not to get caught up in worrying about the things we have and the things we want to accumulate. The things we consume can consume us. Jesus reminded his listeners that God "knows that you need all these things. But strive first for the kingdom of God and his righteousness, and all these things will be given to you as well" (Matthew 6:32-33). In other words, focus on loving, forgiving, and serving the needs of others—knowing that, through Christ, you have been made right with God, and rescued from sin and death.

The apostle Paul spoke about hope in a powerful way in Romans 8, beginning with a question: "If God is for us, who is against us?" (Romans 8:31). God gave up Jesus for us, so God won't hold back anything to save us. Then Paul asked, "Who will separate us from the love of Christ? Will hardship, or distress, or persecution, or famine, or nakedness, or peril, or sword?" (8:35). That covers just about anything we might face in life.

Put God's priorities first

- What kinds of things might separate us from God?

Paul continued, "No, in all these things we are more than conquerors through him who loved us. For I am convinced that neither death, nor life . . . nor anything else in all creation, will be able to separate us from the love of God in Christ Jesus our Lord" (8:37-39). What a promise that is! Hope for today and hope for the future. Does that mean we will never worry about the future again? Probably not. We're human, after all. But God created us, and through Jesus Christ, God saves us. Because of this, the greatest story is a story filled with hope from beginning to end.

Nothing can separate us from the love of God

- What gives you hope? What do you hope for?

PICTURING THE STORY

As you watch the story unfold in the video, reflect on these questions:

- What questions do you have about what it means to live as a follower of Jesus?
- What ideas or concepts interest you most? Which are most challenging?
- What more do you want to know about the story of Jesus? About the New Testament in general?
- For you, what is the most important message you have heard?
- If you could ask Jesus one thing right now, what would it be?
- What's next? What part of the greatest story do you want to explore?

SINGING AND PRAYING THE STORY

The book of Psalms found in the Bible was the worship book of the people of Israel. The psalms are prayers and songs used to offer praise and thanks to God, ask for God's help, seek God's forgiveness, remember God's actions, and even complain or cry out to God. Christians use the psalms the very same way as we worship and as we reflect on our relationship with God.

Psalm 65
A hymn of praise to God.
What is the psalmist thanking God for? What would you add to this prayer of thanks?

Psalm 136
A liturgical prayer celebrating God's faithfulness.
How does this psalm drive home the themes in this chapter? If you were to add your own line or two to the psalm, what would you want to say?

MARK IT

Choose one or more of the following passages from today's section of the story to read during the coming week. Mark your reading using the marking method shown here.

Matthew 5:3-12

Colossians 3:12-17

1 Corinthians 15:35-58

1 Peter 1:3-12

Marking Your Bible

Make notes about the questions and insights you have as you read your Bible. The following symbols might be helpful.

∗   A chapter or verse important to me
!   A new idea
√   A passage to memorize
?   Something not clear to me
∞   God's love
℗   A promise from God
≈   Something that connects with my experience
†   My relationship with God
↔   My relationships with others

Next Time

We've come to the end of this particular journey through the greatest story. But don't stop here. Keep the journey going. Continue to explore the Bible on your own, perhaps taking a different route or following a different road map. Also look for ways to explore the Bible with others. Keep asking: "What's next? What more do I want to discover?" The best way to do that is with others who are asking similar questions.

In the meantime, consider exploring the following articles in *Lutheran Study Bible*:

• Martin Luther on the Bible, pages 1521-1529
• What Should We Expect When We Read the Bible?, pages 1544-1546
• The Bible and God's Mission, pages 1547-1552